A Thousand Paths to Creativity

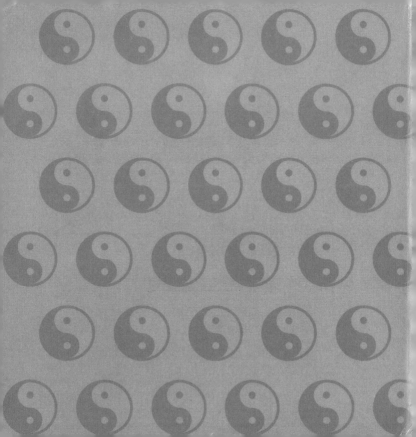

A Thousand Paths to
creativity

David Baird

MQP

Contents

Introduction

Today, perhaps more than at any other time in history, the pressure is on us all to be more creative. This extends into our private lives, the design of our homes and interiors, our methods of parenting, the way we look and dress, how we handle our finances and market ourselves, right down to what's in our garden and what we serve at the dining table.

In our professional lives, with the incredible advances in technology and increased competition, the demand is to be creative on our feet, to produce outstanding results on ever tightening deadlines—often at the drop of a hat. From the factory floor to the executive suite, business relies upon the creativity of every facet of its structure and sometimes we can't see the wood for the trees.

But rest assured, the creativity we seek, the creativity that is needed, is within us all and there for the taking. Whether an individual, a small business, or a global enterprise, the rules and philosophy of creativity are the same. Within these pages are a thousand little motivational keys with which to wind your creative mechanism and get things running as smoothly as clockwork. Wow yourself, and wow the world, with your creativity.

Coming to Terms with Creativity

Creativity is best defined by two small words, "What if?" Let this be the starting point.

Creativity is a journey— wherever you go, go with all your heart.

Curiosity is the fuel of creativity.

Creativity is the capacity to confirm through action what can be imagined.

Creativity is the license to explore, to try things out, and to get things wrong. If you are going to do something wrong, you might as well enjoy it.

Creativity is about trusting your own instincts, and if working in a team, the instincts of others.

Creativity thrives upon disturbance, imbalance, and fluctuation. Unfortunately these are also the three prime dreads of most organizations.

Where does creativity end?
It does not. It merely changes.
We reach the point of change
—we pass through.

**Imagine how repetitive
life would become, how
smothered with sameness
our world would be, were
it not for creativity.**

When you can see what everybody else has seen but be thinking what nobody else has thought, you will have discovered your creativity.

The world's wisdom and the experience of the ages has been preserved through man's creativity.

If you are going to make a living on the proceeds of your creativity it's better to grow a thick skin than to buy an expensive suit.

In creativity there is as much, if not more, to be gained from the journey as there is from reaching the destination.

Wherever possible, encourage creativity in others, not with the aim of developing everyone as inventors and artists, but ensuring a continued balance in this world of critical thinkers.

Creativity can only survive desperation when it is prepared to leave behind everything it ever believed in.

If necessity is the mother of invention, its opposite is the father of creativity.

The secret to creativity is knowing how to select and hide your sources.

Artists are rarely satisfied people. They like it this way. Their creativity is fueled by unrest and dissatisfaction, which makes them stand out from everybody else, and which is why they appear to be more alive than all the rest.

Caution in creativity is often fatal.

One may establish one's creativity by being prepared not only to experiment with ideas but also to take as many of them as possible through to their solutions before presenting them to others.

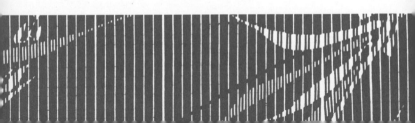

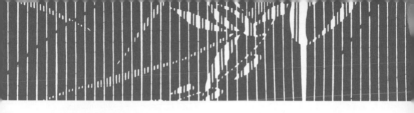

The best place to begin the quest for creativity is the moment you wake on a new day. Tell yourself that anything is possible, then get up and see what is.

Without tension and skepticism, creativity would be far less appealing— and far more predictable.

The first step toward creativity is to acknowledge and accept that by applying ourselves, we can improve and even expand our ability to be creative.

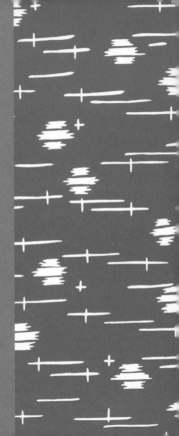

**It takes the greatest creativity of all
to profit from one's mistakes.**

Creativity lets go of certainties
and jumps into the deep end.

**Knowledge and integrity give
creativity its strength and usefulness.**

Creativity is less to do with
intellect than man's play instinct.

**Integrity is vital, for creativity
without integrity is often dreadful
and potentially dangerous.**

Creativity generates
mistakes. True art is
knowing which ones
are worth correcting.

**True creativity illuminates what,
without it, would never have been.**

Man is the only creature to leave behind him traces of his creativity.

Go into the garden of creativity with praise and encouragement and it will bloom all around you. But enter with criticism and discouragement and it will wither before your eyes.

Creativity creates exceptions, and becoming one of these can be a blessing mixed with glory and pain.

For creativity to flourish one should try to look at everything as though it were being seen for the first or the last time.

**The act of
creativity
can solve
almost any
problem.**

Nothing
encourages
creativity
more than the
opportunity it
provides to
fall flat on
one's face.

Creativity is not a spontaneous act. It must be set alight and constantly fueled.

One should always reject coercion, particularly where creativity is concerned. Practice using the mind and its ideas to persuade without force or ultimatum.

Chance is a powerful aspect of creativity. It is like fishing in an unknown pool where the fish always bite.

Creativity, not wars, will provide the vision required to save a world hell-bent on its own destruction.

Creativity not only invigorates, it rebalances and energizes mankind.

Creativity learns nothing until it can give up every preconceived notion and sit down before nature as a child.

Creativity is fluid—it runs from moment to moment, a river of possibilities running into a sea of potential.

True creativity procures the greatest happiness, inspiration, or motivation for the greatest numbers.

Creativity is the only place outside of religion where man might be tempted to be restrained by fear of punishment or hope of reward after death.

Creativity is the greatest of enterprises humankind may engage itself in. Unlike science, to which it is akin, it is beyond reproach if unable to answer all the questions that are put to it. And here ships may fly and nothing need be what it appears to have been designed for.

Frequent repetition may bring happiness but it does not guarantee creativity.

Creativity suffers because the world will always find the genuinely new threatening.

Creativity seeks to simultaneously meet the criteria for the brief while gaining the creative approval of its peers.

Creativity is a practice, an application. The moment we engage such creative practice as research we are in danger of affecting it as a process and the resultant creativity is likely to be flawed.

One must not feel compelled to impose upon our creativity methods that are in retreat purely for the sake of tradition.

Not all creativity should be seen as a discipline bound by process and the relation of form to content. Pure creativity exists outside of these boundaries in the instant and the infinite.

Creativity doesn't always recognize talent, yet talent instantly recognizes genius.

Time was created after the beginning of the universe that God (allegedly) created. If mankind was created by God, in God's image, then we too must create time for our own creativity.

For some, life imitates creativity. For others, life is creativity.

Nothing matches bathing in man's creativity as a means for uplifting the soul.

Creativity loves life.

Creativity takes great pleasure and inspiration from even the smallest offerings.

The secret of creativity is that those who have gone off in search of it have ended up discovering themselves.

Mankind is guilty of constantly setting himself low standards and then consistently failing to achieve them. Creativity is the greatest motivator of man's actions. Inspire his desire to create and he is capable of wondrous things.

A fundamental key to creativity is assiduous and frequent questioning.

In creativity, even in a puddle one can seem at first to be out of one's depth.

Creativity should bring joy into the room, not bring joy when it leaves the room.

In creativity there is no
such thing as a "has-been,"
only "won't-bes" and
"never-wasers."

Creativity must find itself. It lives in the half of the brain that the other half is constantly seeking.

Creativity is like the cream in a bottle of milk—with time and patience it rises to the top.

In creativity the process is far more important than the fame it wins. Fame is just a momentary bubble, empty.

Creativity must learn to understand human needs, for doing so is half the job of meeting them.

In creativity one should never wait until thirst hits before starting to dig the well.

One does not one day suddenly create oneself into creativity. One gets there by learning how to stand, to walk, then run, then dance, and then fly.

It takes as much creativity to understand as it does to make oneself understood.

That which is essential, even if invisible to the eye, is seen in the heart of those who have unlocked their creativity.

We are the captains
of our creativity
and the masters
of our fate.

**Creativity has its own behavior,
which sometimes leads to
certain situations. At this stage
the art comes into play—the
art of talking oneself out of
the situation.**

In business one measures success by the position one achieves over a lifetime. In creativity success is measured by the number of obstacles one has overcome to achieve something.

In creativity, like athletics, one can always rely on the backup of what is termed "second wind."

The aim is to run fast and far enough on your first wind until you discover that just when it feels that all has been spent a surge of energy manifests itself sufficiently to carry you across the finishing line.

Whatever you dream
you can do is probably
something you can do.

The magic of creativity kicks into play when you begin to take action.

All too often we allow those things that we cannot do to interfere with those things that we can actually do.

Hunches are creativity's way of trying to tell us something.

Who can look at the vast spectacle of the sky, the sun, or a crescent moon without feeling stirred to creativity?

Creativity,
like
change,
is not only
necessary
to life,
it is life.

Creativity sees no question as being too foolish to ask, let alone answer.

Creativity in isolation is heart-withering. It must by necessity have the reaction of other hearts or else shrivel away undetected, a pathetic echo of its former self.

Creativity should come with deliberation—not from deliberation.

At the core of creativity lies an awareness of the inherent difficulties. This is counterweighted with the confidence that by persisting and remaining patient there will come a worthwhile result.

Creativity wastes nothing. All life's sorrows and setbacks, difficulties and obstacles are stockpiled and called upon at will.

Creativity is about rearranging knowledge. It takes what exists to bring other hitherto nonexistent things into existence.

One must never expect worthwhile creativity to happen without effort. Failure must not be ascribed to misfortune, neither to lack of inspiration or ability. Blame must be squarely laid at our own feet for insufficient application.

There is no greater crime toward creativity than knowing in the back of our mind what we ought to be doing and ignoring it.

If you want to witness true creativity observe children under ten years of age whose imaginations are running wild — here lies true organic thinking. Nothing added and nothing taken away.

Creativity is least successful when it sets out to try to please everyone.

Creative people bear more scars than medals.

The first step to successful creativity is showing up and making a start.

Mankind by his very nature has a tendency to overcomplicate the simplest things in life. It takes great creativity, however, to make the complicated simple.

Creativity not only knows what to do, but also why to do it.

Creativity must be constantly fed inspiration and new ideas. This means a constant foraging through history and through nature.

Creativity is the ability to connect that which is seemingly unconnected.

Creativity takes
conviction.
And a lot of
solutions.

In creativity the balance between benefits and defects is more easily improved by removing defects than by increasing benefits.

Desire is the fuel
of creativity.

Creativity allows us to see the opportunities that lie in the midst of difficulties. Creativity is doomed when approached with a fear of failure.

There is great wisdom to be found in creativity, while knowledge has become blurred by too much information.

A rational mind is often better favored above an intuitive mind, as it is considered to serve its owner better. Yet the intuitive mind is the gateway to adventures in creativity, and should be considered a gift.

On the scale of creativity, imagination far outweighs knowledge.

Creativity is the ability to manage one's imagination.

Creativity is the well that exists deep within our subconscious. Only when we learn to reach it can we draw from its clear waters.

Creativity is a different way of thinking. In music it is thought using sound.

Creativity is rarely swift, nor does it often come easy.

Nothing clears away the dust of everyday life from the soul better than the winds of creativity.

Creativity suffers when it sets out to find perfect solutions in what is, after all, an imperfect world.

The creative ideas agonizingly forged by an individual often outshine the creative output of a group.

Creativity is the license to try things out whether they ultimately work or not.

Reflection is essential to creativity—it allows us the necessary space and time to question what already exists, to think, to daydream, and to ponder.

Vision alone is but a dream, but when put into action it can achieve wondrous things.

Creativity is a marriage of vision and action.

Creativity is less successful when it attempts to resolve contradictions than when it embraces those contradictions within its structure.

Creativity asks not that we follow in the footsteps of those who went before us, but that we seek what it was they sought, and make new footprints of our own.

Being puzzled is a condition conducive to creativity.

It is often said that there is a very fine line between genius and insanity. Creativity erases that line.

Creativity must be lead by curiosity—not precedents.

In business, ideas are worth money, yet how many ideas are daily stifled?

Potential millions are lost when managements ignore the fact that when it comes to creativity it is they who must take the first step.

Anyone who seeks a solution that does not involve creativity is embarking upon a futile mission.

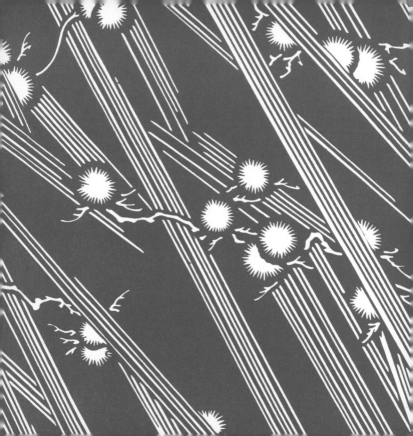

Making the Leap

In each age, men of genius undertake the ascent. From below, the world follows them with their eyes. These men go up the mountain, enter the clouds, disappear, reappear. People watch them, mark them. They walk by the side of precipices. They daringly pursue their road. See them aloft, see them in the distance; they are but black specks. On they go. The road is uneven, its difficulties constant. At each step, a wall, at each step a trap. As they rise the cold increases. They must

make their ladder, cut the ice and walk
on it, hewing the steps in haste.
A storm is raging. Nevertheless they
go forward in their madness. The air
becomes difficult to breath. The abyss
yawns below them. Some fall. Others
stop and retrace their steps; there is a
sad weariness. The bold ones
continue. They are eyed by the eagles;
the lightning plays about them:
the hurricane is furious. No matter,
they persevere.

Victor Hugo

Developing new solutions and ideas requires a great deal of creative thought. To become more creative one must be willing, and able, to transform one's ways of thinking.

Imagination is the place to see the big picture. It's the place where decisions and their consequences can be considered, where all possibilities exist, and choices must be made.

Not all old maps will lead us to the new lay of the land. And new maps may lead us too far away from the old lay of the land.

Creativity often leads down dark, unlit corridors that go to nowhere certain. Those too afraid of the dark to explore these areas of life will have to suffice with imitation—and will never reach their true creative potential.

Don't rush into things—ponder your decisions and their potential consequences. What sometimes appears to be logical is often not practical.

Risk is inherent in all creativity, and the art is knowing when to take it.

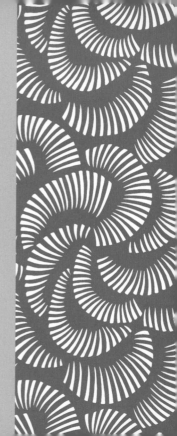

Never deny the present in your rush to face the future, for the future is shaped by the here and now. The present is the new frontier, and it took a great many pioneers to reach it.

Creativity is the greatest advocate of Doing. But it also requires periods of inactivity in order for things to occur to us.

One can spend forever failing
to predict the future, or
knuckle down to creating it.

Thought produces thought and
thought purges thought.
Creative thought produces
imaginative thoughts different to
our habitual everyday thoughts.
These are the unusual thoughts
that lead to creativity.

Things are there to be tried, and unless we try them how will we ever get to know whether or not they work?

We carry with us at any time the most sophisticated piece of technology that exists—the human mind. It is this that dreamed up and made possible everything from the safety pin to interplanetary travel.

Unless we carry beauty with us we can never hope to create beauty, just as a factory needs to retool to deal with new ideas. So we must begin to see our mind in the same way and retool our ways of thinking to produce new ideas.

Creativity thrives in an atmosphere of freedom and democracy.

Creativity has a tendency to surprise until it manifests in some wondrous thing. There is no outward sign. The soul looketh steadily forwards creating a new world before her, leaving worlds behind her.

Ralph Waldo Emerson

The power of creativity is enough to pull everything into order.

Through the power of our ideas we create our world: if we are actors, musicians, or artists we create our audiences; if we are writers we create our readers; in business we create our customers and our suppliers. We are responsible for our entire creative landscape.

Creativity asks: "What do we know?" And: "What do we need to know?" Questions are needed in order to produce answers.

Business and industry often come unstuck when they prescribe too many rules and measures to creativity. They rarely feel secure enough to give it its head. Innovation is the fastest horse in the race—if the jockey just lets go of the reins it can win.

It is not enough to point at someone and say, "Be innovative." We must also give them an insight as to what they are expected to achieve, and the constraints under which they are to create it.

Almost everything we encounter is based upon action and reaction in business, arts, sport, politics, indeed everywhere. When we see the competition's innovation we feel the need to react—they lead, we follow.

Just consider for a moment what is the key component of any organization, company, business, or team: its people and their creative powers to innovate. Recognize this and innovation need no longer be merely a consequential reaction.

Every team, business, or organization is its own laboratory— the whole shebang—not tucked away secretly in a room in the basement or the entire 17th floor.

Innovation on a company or organizational level is dependent upon absolutely every speck of its human resources, from the cafeteria staff to the CEO. They are all there to serve the vision and if they do, the vision will serve them.

If we are to get beyond imitation into the realm of innovation, before we even put on our thinking caps, we have to isolate ourselves from the freebies and put in some elbow grease.

What is it that gives some staying power while others go to the wall or fall silently unnoticed from their thrones? The power to invent and reinvent.

What places anyone in an advantage point above their competitors is the ability to reach a state of continuous creativity and innovation—like the boxer who can suddenly switch to fighting southpaw at will or the football team who appear to reinvent their game as they go along.

Before innovation can be released, the work environment must first give its blessing. Until then, only the potential to innovate exists.

The mind can proceed only so far upon what it knows and can prove. There comes a point where the mind takes a higher plane of knowledge, but can never prove how it got there. All great discoveries have involved such a leap.

Albert Einstein

It's never too late when you've got the power to innovate.

Innovation needs the flexibility and freedom to operate outside of the rules. To develop new ways of thinking one must also develop new ways of working.

Ideas of high potential are worthless in an unsuitable context.

To be smart in business we need to think beyond today to what people will need and want in the future—and how we can take what it is we do to that point and still hold our own.

One can rest assured that one can master today, but never ignore the need to be able to master tomorrow.

Innovation and creativity can lead to invention of course, but they can also lead us to seeing new uses and new ways that others may never have seen or considered before.

The capacity for creative innovation, once developed, places its possessors in a state of advantage—and the benefits will be reaped for a very long time.

Create time.

Create a work of art.

Create a product.

Create a niche.

Create interest.

Create a market.

Create value.

Create profit.

It is true that not everyone possesses what it takes to become an inventor, but we all have it within us to become more creative and innovative people.

People who have only one choice really don't have any choice at all.

When we are able to tap into our creative potential we can apply it to the way we think, and subsequently everything we do.

Creativity can't sit still. From hotpants to paintings of cans of soup, three-wheeled cars to buildings that reach the clouds—if man can think of it and create it, the need and the desire for it will follow.

Creative strategies constantly reshape our world. With these every day is filled with surprises.

Things don't fail because of the marketplace, they fail when we, especially our leaders, are not up to the task.

Not using our creativity is like owning a Ferrari and using it to plow fields.

Ideas are not solutions. They are thoughts, suggestions, hunches, and opinions that must be put into action and worked through, before they can be applied as solutions.

One cannot expect a creative team or individual to adhere to a strict plan and be innovative. Creativity requires support from partners, bosses, players, and staff if it is to be developed to its full potential.

Ask yourself: "Do you nurture or kill off creativity in your place of work?"

Ask yourself: "Do you nurture or kill off creativity in your day-to-day life?"

Ask yourself: "Do you go out of your way to positively encourage creativity in others?"

Look to any organization that has stumbled and you are likely to find a history of squelched creativity.

Creativity challenges everything. It is an essential quality of its nature. It must get beyond the paradigms of order, imposed procedure, and even tradition in order to become effective.

To a creative cook there are infinite possibilities for preparing the exact same ingredients. Were they to work to instructions there would be only one.

Creative thinking is vital if we are to maximize the value we can get from existing resources.

Creative thinking is vital if we are to minimize the effect of our actions upon the environment.

Creative thinking is vital if we are to maximize the positive effect of our decisions on the world at large.

When we are told how to think we end up not thinking for ourselves at all.

With freedom one can develop shortcuts to deliberate or impromptu creative thinking—most effective when facing time and budgetary constraints.

Our creativity offers us a shortcut toward unraveling those lessons it is important for us to learn from and those that offer little or nothing to our lives or the task in hand.

Creative people trust their instincts, and those wishing to benefit through the creativity of others must learn to trust the instincts of creative people.

For individuals to develop their creativity and creative thinking it is vital that they place themselves within a sphere where creative reasoning is viewed as important and is positively encouraged.

Some use computers to enhance creative thinking skills while others use thinking skills to improve computer creativity.

Bravely make room within your schedule to research, for research's sake, and explore the development of reasoning skills within the creative process.

It is important not to lose touch with our successful creative experiences. These will help us to draw vital conclusions that can enable us to meet the needs of new projects with less risk.

Cast your net far and wide and seek out examples of "guided thinking." Apply these to your own historical perspective and consider the benefits while remaining open to the possibilities of a guided creative process for future application.

Sometimes it is important to restructure our creative processes if we are to improve upon our thinking and reasoning faculties.

Creative communities sow ideas and harvest solutions.

In creativity there are always two parallel bodies of research: one is your own individual research in terms of your creative methodology in relation to immediate demands; the other relates directly to the project in hand.

Creative communities encourage cooperative exploration above adversarial thinking.

Every failure contains hidden assets. If one can face up to it and study it imaginatively it will provide the raw information for new creativity.

Perseverance and determination are the handmaidens of creative success. With these we can endure anything that comes along, survive the knocks and the storms, and reach journey's end.

It takes a discerning creative eye to see the divine sense that lies in madness and the madness that lies in much of what is considered to be good sense.

Creativity should not be limited to grand schemes—concentrate too on common, everyday problems.

Whenever mankind has offered his vision for new possibilities for the human race, these have been branded as being utopian ideas. Creative utopia exists too—wherever we dare attempt to change the status quo.

He who can draw connections between the ostensibly unrelated is the one who will make creative breakthroughs.

Creativity links every moment—past, present, and future— in a moment of transition distilled from good and evil, forged from cause and effect.

Creative valor grows by daring— fear grows when we hold ourselves back.

To separate the creator from his creativity is like trying to separate the future from the past.

Everyone has a point of view. Creativity tolerates each and accepts them as challenges to its own understanding.

Optimism brings confidence to everything we create. We reach its state by immersing ourselves in positive thoughts armed with the power to nurture and the power to heal.

Tell yourself this: "I am the creator of my life; I am the creator of my world."

Meet daily challenges with confidence, grace, and a creative outlook.

When our creative ideas are powerful enough, some of them rub off even on our most vehement challengers.

Life's challenges exist to help us discover who we are creatively.

A gifted creative team reaches the top by climbing a ladder with ideas for rungs and framed with bold efforts and strong instincts.

Being wrong early on is better than being right far too late.

Creativity plunges us right into the thick of life to a place where everything becomes interesting.

Being creative is about being prudent enough to see the difficulties while at the same time being bold enough to see the advantages. By seeing both, one can diminish the former, embrace the latter, and win through.

Creative confidence is not to be confused with creative arrogance. The former is greeted as decent and bold, the latter considered unfriendly and vulgar.

Being creative and never starting is no different to being uncreative.

Creativity demands perseverance, but perseverance without talent is like sitting down to eat a bowl of soup with a fork.

A creative life tends to draw good and interesting things toward it.

A creative strategy is useless unless you are willing and able to adapt it.

We need to apply our creative ability. Just as the body benefits from exercise, we need to put aside time to regularly exercise our creative thinking.

The creative soul is the place we reach into for our ideas. Sometimes they are given willingly and other times we must wrench them from their stronghold.

One must be prepared to accept that we all have it within us to be more creative.

When you know where your questions are leading the answers come to you.

Once we embark on the path toward creativity we must continue through life seeking out opportunities to be more creative in our work and day-to-day lives.

With each new creative departure one should leave with two pieces of luggage—the desire to have fun, and the desire to discover as much as possible along the way.

With each creative departure there follows a creative arrival.

If one wishes to witness the potential of creativity, observe children: not so much their results and achievements, but their cognitive processes.

We all have our creative mountains to climb, we can go it alone and struggle, or accept a little help from below.

Creativity does not come ready-made, it is an infinite system to be applied to an infinite variety of situations.

One doesn't merely give over one's creativity to a project, each project requires that we give over our entire life.

For creativity to fly it is essential to exorcise several little nagging demons—the ones that tell us not to say anything that will cause embarrassment and the ones that tell us not to do anything that might meet with disapproval.

We are all different only in years and experience. Learn to respect the intelligence, integrity, and the creative capacity for deep thought and hard work, which are latent somewhere in everyone.

Stop looking at creativity as a gulf or rift—it is a bridge, and a vital means of sharing.

Creative people are ordinary human beings, who give their all, their time, respect, attention, and love to the task at hand and who expect nothing more than payment in kind.

It is creativity that gives the means of expression to those who would describe creativity as therapy or something to satisfy the ego.

We should all develop the capacity to change rapidly and frequently or risk losing our place.

Think up new things. Do new things. Embrace change.

A business must constantly reinvent itself in order to remain competitive, not necessarily in what it does or manufactures, but in the way it is perceived and the appeal it generates.

Occasionally focus on, and define for yourself, your past and present creative approaches.

A culture of creative innovation should be the goal of every nation as it will benefit not only its own people but all mankind.

Creativity asks that we seek to constantly develop our personal ability to grow.

Creativity is not limited to galleries or factories. It can be effectively applied to everything we do, to all living, learning, and working environments regardless of size or status.

Allow your
creativity
to nourish
yourself as well
as others.

There is all around us, depending upon how we choose to perceive it, either an overwhelming universe—or a universe of possibilities.

The
Wider View

Creativity must analyze not only the unknown but the obvious too.

Imagine the level of creativity possible if people's egos didn't get in the way and no one minded who gets the credit.

Creative people view the future as something to be equally distributed between everyone.

Violence is not creative.

Vanity is not creative.

Self-love is not creative.

Difficulty is one of creativity's greatest attributes.

Creative experience must be undergone—it cannot be manufactured.

We must learn to differentiate between generosity and charity.

Inside all of us, in the midst of our winters, are glorious summer days.

It is one thing to be blind, and quite another to be so blind as to never listen.

Consider Rudyard Kipling whose writings were at first rejected and Elvis Presley who was thought to be a dud, going nowhere.

Where would creativity be without the capacity to greet and change one's standpoint? At the beginning of the 1980s the creator of the world's most famous operational software believed that 640K of memory would be ample for anybody.

Thank goodness the telephone lived beyond those who initially saw it as having little value to people's lives.

When radio was first invented, funding was difficult to come by as it was considered that people wouldn't be prepared to pay for a communication device where messages were sent to no one in particular.

Each member of a team should be positively encouraged to develop their abilities and grow their talents, for when creativity is sheltered under the same roof as problems the problems soon disappear.

Imagine the doubts and difficulties of convincing the world that one day most people would have a computer in their home.

Thank goodness that data processing outlived those who saw it only as a passing fad.

Where would surgery have gone had it not been for the creative intuition of a dedicated few? Before them it was considered inhumane to open the chest, the brain, or the abdomen.

Today there are many paths to creativity. Sometimes the more informative creations are those that provide us with the substance from which the creator's outlook was developed.

Elizabeth I of England is said to have offered "all my possessions for one moment of time." Who then among us will offer all time for a moment of creativity?

Sometimes one feels compelled to create a monster to subdue a monster. When we do this we become a monster ourselves.

Sometimes we create things that are beyond our skills and we must ask others to fabricate them for us or accept that we must let go of the idea.

Man's wisdom and experience down through the ages are preserved through his creativity.

If you cannot trust the one who has proved it then you are incapable of trusting anyone.

Seek to use your intellect and rely less upon your memory.

Become a doer of things, not one who seeks to get the credit for them.

What is the point in generating ideas if one is too nervous to embrace them?

No matter if there is not enough time to do it right the first time, there is always time to do it again.

To discover new creative possibilities, one must be able to raise new questions.

The world's creative output would slow to a halt if we were all to stop adapting other people's ideas.

Creative genius has the faculty of perceiving in a nonhabitual way.

It is better to remain silent and be thought a fool than to open one's mouth and remove all doubt.

Too many imaginations discard the old. The creative imagination must hold old questions and problems in high regard—inspiring new possibilities, new approaches, and new advances.

The chief glory of mankind is the capacity to create.

Why fear thought? It is free to everyone who seeks to use it yet we seem content to view it only as a subversive, destructive revolutionary force to be quelled in others.

What is coercion? It is an attempt to restrain or dominate others by nullifying individual will, and to compel them to carry out a particular act or make a certain choice enforced by force or threat. The creative individual must reject the use of coercion, and prevent himself from being coerced and thereby achieve creative freedom.

Imagination points us in the direction that leads to what we might yet discover or create.

One should not fear
creating slowly but one
should be very afraid
of standing still.

Our lives are filled with vagaries
and generalities but we must
be creative in detail.

It is far easier to achieve reality by remaining detached from it.

Every exit is an entry somewhere else.

Tom Stoppard

Creativity is fueled by questions. When we cease asking questions, we become fools.

When we choose to lead creative lives we need never again fear boredom.

What is the beginning of creativity? Imagination.

While we busy ourselves creating this world our children are occupied inventing a better one.

Only a fool or a suicide would jump from an airplane without a parachute. The same goes for anyone foolish enough to attempt being creative without first thinking about what they are doing.

Inspiration comes to us from who knows where, like a memory of something we've yet to experience.

Pay attention to silence and let it carry you to your deepest inner reaches, the very core of your being where life is reflected.

Inspiration lies on the flip side of self-consciousness.

The wonderful thing about creativity is that one can deep-freeze one's ideas and thaw them out at any time for future use.

Where does creative inspiration spring from? The mystical view is that there is some form of supernatural or universal force above and beyond us channeling our thoughts and directing our actions.

Creativity needn't be a struggle, but creative people often choose to let it become one.

Creative people cannot afford to be rigid, else like the brittle branch, they snap with the slightest breeze. One must become fluid and featherlight.

Creativity does not exist in a vacuum; it must be sparked by outside contact.

Dreams are fragmented.
Creative visionaries dream
the whole picture.

Successful businesses do not practice
coercion, they encourage imagination
and harvest the fruits of imagination.
They create a sort of creative
permaculture that is both self-sufficient
and self-perpetuating.

The most important resource to the human race is creativity. Without it there would be no progression, and with it there will always be hope.

Those who consider themselves to be always right are usually the ones with no original ideas whatsoever.

Creative lives are landscaped with peaks and troughs. One strives for the peaks, but it is from those valleys that the really great things are seen.

Creative people inevitably work out
how to make something possible.
The impossible just takes a little longer.

**If a sufficiently dedicated and
patient effort should prove
unproductive, then one must
prepare one's mental, physical, and
experiential resources to move on,
either temporarily or permanently,
to other creative problems.**

Leave room for trial and error and
always some time for play.

Inside each of us is a child
that still wants to play—this
is our creative desire.

One can sit and contemplate grasping
the bull by the horns but one really
does need to eventually get up and
physically do something about it.

God forbid that we should
quell our curiosity for it is the
mainspring of our creativity.

Every person, at least once in their lifetime, should try to prove something they imagined.

The closest parallel to the process of creativity is the process of learning.

Perhaps we can best view our creativity as the coming together of our desire to do something, our knowledge of what or why to do it, and our skills for how to do it.

All the components of our learning, imagination, and experience must be given free rein to work together if we are to establish good creative habits.

Try this: look, now see what it is you are looking at. Then try to understand what it is that you see. Learn from what it is that you understand, then act on what you have learned.

Perhaps creativity is a form of striving for immortality now that so many no longer believe in an afterlife.

Place yourself in situations that test your conviction to what you propose as actions and solutions.

One of the recognizable facets of creative people is their playful mental flexibility. They have within them the ability to keep probing for a solution to a problem while always remaining open to alternatives.

Experiment with your creative perception and develop your shortcuts to understanding.

Experiment with the transferring of relevant information, and develop through experimentation how it is that you comprehend information.

Creativity has many guides and systems, but in truth, when the hour arrives to create, most are cast aside and instinct takes over.

Creativity will always remain mysterious to us because the defining conditions under which it occurs are unexpectedness and unpredictability.

A key trait of creative people is their dogged persistence as they strive to reach their goals.

If I create from the heart, nearly everything works; if from the head almost nothing.

Marc Chagall

Try to relax—let go of your hold on your mind and let it wander and explore.

Creative coercion violates the natural rhythms of creativity.

Creative people tend to be objectively critical and will discover faults where they exist.

Time must be allowed for one's ideas to incubate.

Increase the odds in one's favor to ensure that creativity does occur through the preparation of a favorable setting for creative chance.

Until one is committed, there is hesitancy and the chance to draw back from creativity. There are no guarantees with creativity.

Good creative practice begins with preparation, the groundwork, a period of collation, gathering one's thoughts, stockpiling and inputting ideas, images, impressions, and inspirations.

Next follows a drifting period in which one lets go of all certainties. Some call this a period of incubation where thoughts and ideas sit like newly sown seeds, until some begin to take root and sprout their first growth. Think of this as floating above oyster beds.

Next comes a period of creative intervention, a time to go into action and see if ideas can be proven. Think of this as total immersion in the creative project, or diving for pearls.

Nothing is as invigorating as that moment which is the prelude to a period of high creativity.

The birth of a creative idea is beautiful. It begins unseen, felt from within, a palpable thing so real the mind knows it even before it takes earthly form.

An altered state of consciousness marks the birth of a new idea.

Once you have the impulse to create, it takes control and must be served.

Research smooths the way for the creative process.

Never underestimate the immense therapeutic value of becoming involved in creative pursuits.

A good artist would not necessarily make a good scientist or a good businessperson. Artistic creativity has its constraints provided from within, the constraints of science and business come from the external reality of a logical formal world.

Within everyone there is latent creativity just waiting to be unlocked, and the key to freeing it is to allow your mind to become more flexible than it is now.

Maximizing preparation maximizes the likelihood of creativity.

It has been estimated that at any given time we only use between 10 percent and 15 percent of our mental capacity.

When we are being creative and generating good ideas, it not only energizes us, but it also becomes profitable.

Seek out methods of expanding your mind—this has a remarkable way of accelerating one's creative potential.

Once stimulated, the desire to reach beyond one's present boundaries is the very essence of creative attitude.

It is little wonder that creativity is rarely called upon in the "real world" as most managers, leaders, and bosses would find it too big a gamble to become dependent upon it for success, particularly after considering the vagaries of chance.

Creativity is the desire to reach for new horizons.

Creative insight is that moment when out of the blue we suddenly come up with the answer.

If we were to use structured sequential thought as with reading, writing, and most forms of arithmetic then we would only ever use half of our brain. Creativity employs logical, analogical, and lateral thought and exercises many parts of the brain, including the right side, which is considered to be the seat of insight.

Every creative medium has its own constraints.

Without preparation, creativity is rather like returning over and over again to the same place to search for something you have lost.

If one wishes to witness creativity happening in real time then a visit to the performing arts is what's required—here creativity is externalized for all to see.

Many creators of performance tend to choose a preferred set of constraints within which they strive to create innovations.

There can be no
creative constraints
without preparation.

Creativity
thrives on
problems.

The problems upon
which creativity thrives
require constraints in
order to exist.

Why should it be that creative insights are often provoked by encountering an anomaly or through observing the failure of existing solutions?

Business demands action and rarely understands that action does not lead to creativity. Creativity must consolidate ideas, visions, dreams, and imagination and these things lead to plans, which lead to action.

Creative freedom may have more to do with what you are than what it is you do.

Sometimes the expected unexpectedly fails to work leading us in new creative directions.

An act of creativity becomes an act of memory when it is driven purely by intuition and aesthetics.

Is creativity a state or a trait?

When we term someone a creative genius it would appear that we are talking about someone who, rather inexplicably and repeatedly, seems able to make intuitive conjectures that subsequently turn out to be right, even if at the time of creating they are not able to produce proof.

Creative perception is a form of pre-verbal, aesthetic intuition—we know before we do, we do before we speak.

When stood against what already exists, something creative has immediate value. When it is perceived as being needed, its value increases.

Nothing can bring mankind closer in common to the creation of the universe than his own acts of creativity.

Why, if given the same initial knowledge or skill, do some people take flight and make original contributions while others remain fruitless?

Creativity, like science, must ask itself if it is possible to generate and recognize new and valuable outcomes without having sufficient command of what is already available.

Shaping
Ourselves

Everything that is was once only imagined.

Many complain that they have reached a creative roadblock. The answer here is simply to take a detour.

The ability to think creatively strengthens us as individuals by enhancing our natural talents.

In every creative process there is a path to be discovered if one is to be free to gather momentum—it is the path of least resistance.

It is no good working hard and striving to do your best if you do not have some concept of what it is you are working on, and a creative approach toward it.

Most creative ideas that have excelled started out as ideas considered too absurd for words.

One should not become
confused between being
constructive and being creative.
A construction is only adored
after it is completed.
A creation is adored even
before it exists.

Imagination is the route
to everything we might
yet create, or discover
along the way.

Of course there are often rational solutions to problems. Creative problem-solving, however, adopts less rational processes of finding them.

There is more to be learned from our mistakes or from following our own wrong assumptions than there is to be discovered at any fountain of wisdom.

If something is worthwhile, it should be done right. Take the time to get the results you really want.

A creative mind
will always survive
bad advice.

To be creative one must not fear the accidental. Sometimes it is best to empty oneself completely of all preconceptions.

Most creative processes become threatened at some stage by bottlenecks, and one must develop the knack of relieving these as and when they appear.

When it comes to information there is no better source to turn to than nature.

To be famously creative one should try to learn from the insights of other famous creative people down through the ages.

If in doubt,
dream.

Creativity is always on the lookout.

Creativity doesn't merely wait for inspiration—it goes out of its way to seek inspiration.

Creativity is always exploring its environment.

Take time to reflect—in doing so one generates many thoughts…and many ideas.

Reflecting is the imagination's way of pondering our ideas. And those that survive this quiet questioning are the ones with most potential.

Many of the world's greatest discoveries
have come about through disorder.

The most creative
daydreams begin
with the words,
"What if?"

Never seek shelter from a brainstorm.

One should never be ashamed to borrow ideas from others. Such selective embracing generates new ideas, stimulates decision-making, and leads to invention and innovation.

To be original, strive to be creatively incapable of being imitated by others— even if you yourself have imitated others.

Creative wisdom is being able to evaluate, distinguish among dangers, and make the least harmful decisions.

An idea can only be improved by nurturing. Always remain objective. Constantly evaluate. And never become too precious to reject what will not work.

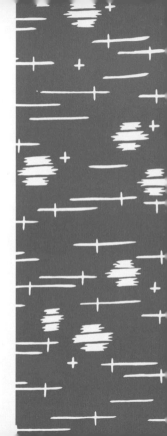

**Working hard is not enough.
Doing your best is not enough.
What is vital is knowing what
to work on.**

A modicum of inaccuracy often
serves to remove the need for
complicated explanation.

**Armed with knowledge and the
desire to create, the first tool
necessary for our task is the
powerful tool of thought—how to
achieve it, and how to control it.**

Trust your creative instincts: people are usually right in their beliefs. Whether they believe that they can, or believe that they can't, who is to say they are wrong?

The world cannot be freeze-framed, nor can it be made stable. Our creativity needs to work outside of the bounds of history and traditional thought that we might face each new tomorrow with creative confidence and the ability to improvise in situations that are entirely new to us.

One should always seek to exercise one's imagination, and never limit it to the extent of its own backyard. This is what separates the adult imagination from children's. We are mature enough to go out beyond the garden gate and play.

Plagiarism is the fertilizer for originality.

The workplace is the hardware store that must provide the tools to enable those who work there to become their best. This is the path to productivity.

When you doubt your contribution, look back through time and you will see that it is individuals and small groups of committed people who have changed the world.

Nothing should be made simpler than possible.

Brainstorming is an ideal way to get a lot of ideas, and in among them is bound to be at least one good one.

Our most daring ideas are like soldiers at war—many are sacrificed that each new battle might be won.

Science has shown that there is increased frontal lobe activity in the brain in people when they recall happy events and decreased frontal lobe activity in people recalling angry or fearful events. This is an important discovery as this is the area of the brain where our executive thinking processes occur.

Nothing fuels the creative being more than the spiritual inspiration derived from discovering that people trust and believe in you.

The word genius should be used as sparingly as salt if one wishes to avoid getting into a pickle.

Inspiration might be described as those moments when we are doing our best, while not knowing what it is we are doing.

The ultimate motivation has to be the deadline.

Inspiration remains stunted when confined to the safe and comfortable. For it to really grow it must be injected with a modicum of risk.

At first there will appear to be many possibilities, often too many, but soon experience will show you that there are few possibilities, often too few.

Brooding is good. It is a form of mental doodling, and it uses less ink.

Every new idea should have at least a moment in which it appears a little crazy.

If a concept is wrong, no number of ideas will put it right.

Imagination is better than memory.

In the middle of difficulty lies opportunity.

Teachers open the door, but you must enter by yourself.

It is perhaps coming to a time when it is no longer enough to make our creativity satisfying to ourselves and with the main aim being to express ourselves.

Well begun
is half done.

**The "silly question" is the
first intimation of some
totally new development.**

Let your creative input be part of the solution, not part of the problem.

Before you create, ask yourself some questions:
Is it necessary?
Will it improve on anything before it?
Is the world likely to want it?

When stuck in a creative rut, one must use all the brains one has—and as many as one can borrow.

Never ignore your dreams—they are your stepping stones to creativity.

The creative mind looks to the past, the present, and the future.

All of us can be creative, it is not difficult. But it is those who can be creative in the right way, for all the right reasons, at the right time, who are truly artists.

Creative management is about motivating people to draw the very best out of themselves— it should not be about merely issuing orders and organizing every single thing.

In order to create well one must first become good at thinking well.

It takes a great deal of savvy to know when it is better not to create. In the public arena this is the equivalent of speaking out when remaining silent would have been better advised.

If I don't agree with you it is not because I have not been listening.

Usually those things that have been created with very little effort are not viewed with pleasure— and are often perceived as having little value or worth.

Creative work should never set out to defend itself against the risk of being seen.

As we gaze into the creative abyss, it gazes back into us.

A distracted person takes two hours to do 60 minutes.

We all go through moments of panic when the pressure is on and inspiration is not forthcoming. It's like standing at a railroad crossing when the barrier is down, the bell is sounding, and the lights are flashing, but there's no sign of the train.

It's one thing having a photographic memory and another to remember to remove the lens cap.

**Get creative.
Go back to nature
for information.**

Get creative.
Live for your
dreams and dream
for your living.

Get creative: learn to forage.
Foraging is gathering
information.

**Get creative: reflect.
Reflecting is an excellent
way of generating ideas.**

Get creative: adopt.
Adopting is selecting an idea.

Get creative: nurture.
Nurturing is improving
upon your idea.

Get creative: knuckle down.
Knuckling down means
never giving up.

Big ideas come in all
shapes and sizes.

**Always be on the lookout
for, and be ready to collect,
new information.**

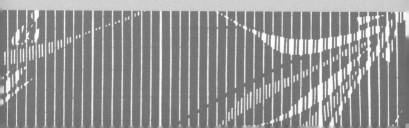

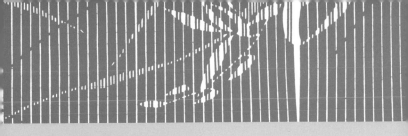

Explore your environment. This is where new ideas are often to be found.

Converse with nature and it will provide inspiration to those who seek it.

Educate your abilities. Only then can you develop them.

The creative brain is like a snow-globe all shaken up. Make small waiting periods, or miniature vacations, periods of consolidation when ideas and fancies can settle in the brain. And when they do so, when things become clear again, move into action.

Forget success or failure and just get on with being creative.

One may always improve upon an idea through nurturing it with objective evaluation and rejection of those aspects that do not work.

Life is an ongoing creative adventure. Whatever our expectations everything can change at the drop of a hat. So remain flexible.

To be creative, we need to accept the free license we are granted at birth to fantasize about being greater than we feel ourselves to be, and then work toward becoming so.

Why are so many people frightened to ask for opportunities to work more creatively?

It is to everybody's advantage to ask for help and support in being creative.

Creative ideas are not solutions but the seeds with which to grow solutions if nurtured properly.

The vast majority prefer to continue doing things as things have always been done, so creative people must be prepared to have their greatest ideas rejected, refused, or even targeted for assassination.

In order to achieve creative freedom one must first come to recognize and understand the differences between coercion, persuasion, and influences.

The right thought captured in the right words has the potential to make the entire world stop and think.

Work stimulates inspiration just as an hors d'oeuvre whets the appetite.

**To do one's best creative work,
when one is not being industrious,
one must also develop the ability
to be very idle.**

The lack of a good idea is a
greater obstacle than the lack
of money.

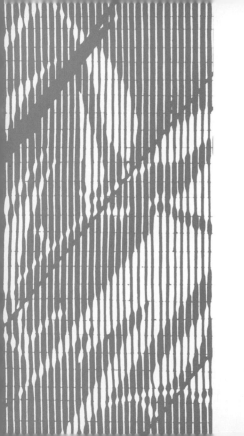

No great
creative
discovery
ever came
to light
without
some
very bold
guesswork.

Ask yourself the big question: is it better to succeed in imitation or risk failing in a bid for originality?

Do not be too quick to condemn those ideas that are considered absurd in one generation, as they may not be deemed so in the next.

Chaos is not to be feared. Where it exists it necessitates the most creative thinking.

It is not necessary to employ coercion to eliminate disorder. If anything, it can only lead to chaos.

Shoes existed long before anyone had the idea of having both a left and a right one.

The problem is the birthplace of beautiful solutions.

Some creative theories are just crazy, and others are just crazy enough to be true.

Better to use one's creative forces than to fight against them.

When two minds begin sparking off of one another the result is pure creative magic.

Whether it is a tree being blown by the wind, a child at play, or a horse in full gallop, a painter will invest time in studying his subject, and in some way enter into its nature before commencing.

When creative thinkers look at the world they see a blank canvas and quickly contact their imagination.

One can wait forever for a creative muse to arrive, or develop the knack of getting in touch with one's own inner child.

People tend to steal old ideas because new ones take just too much effort to try to put across.

Going through life without making any mistakes is a clear sign of a person who never tried to create anything new.

One cannot live a creative life without first letting go of the fear of being wrong.

To the creative the impossible is nothing more than the yet untried.

One must take up arms to defeat habit—this is how originality wins through.

Don't be afraid of new ideas—it is always going along with the old ones we should fear.

In the stillness of meditation the muses arrive. Some of the greatest creative works have been produced in this way.

A creative thinker is not only flexible but adaptable enough and willing to rearrange their thinking.

A good traveler has no fixed plans, and is not intent on arriving.

Lao Tzu

Armed with a creative memory we may have roses in every season.

The cost of delight is paid with our attention.

Most people will go through life only seeing what they are prepared to see. Creative people go through life prepared to see it all.

Considerations

When we are young we feel convinced that we know everything. As we get older we become convinced that we know nothing at all.

Living a creative life is akin to being born anew everyday.

The power of our imagination gives us the potential to transform our world and everything in it.

The only thing available to us in our plight to remain youthful and active is our desire to be creative.

To reach the paths of creative thought, we must first step away from the way we were taught to think at school, which was fine for passing exams but difficult to apply to a creative life.

We are all born with intelligence.
Our mission is to learn how to think for ourselves.

What is human perception if powerless without imagination?

There is no creative person who has not felt a sense of self.

One's life should be spent exploring the finite—only by doing so can we ever hope to proceed beyond it into the infinite.

The mind is a living, growing, inner universe constantly expanding with each new idea.

Great ideas are reward enough to a creative mind. Turned into reality they profit many.

Of course we can all understand One,
And that One and One makes Two.
Only some understand
the importance of AND.

**Which captures more
imaginations—the dream
or the plan?
Martin Luther King said, "I have a
dream," not, "I have this plan."**

Hold on to your dreams—those who dream most, do most.

Why are we creative?
Perhaps it is because in all the animal kingdom, man is the only creature that gets bored.

What you can do, or dream you can, begin it; boldness has genius, power, and magic in it.

Johann Wolfgang von Goethe

Creative thought presents itself to us in a series of images and feelings. These are what we communicate to the world.

It is essential to recognize the common blocks to your creative thinking process and develop the wherewithal to remove them at will, or strategies to get around them.

The world's most creative minds will always survive bad training.
Many will survive despite having no training at all.

In the right hands there is no such thing as a screwball idea—only the potential of wonderful new inventions.

An exploration that ventures away from what we are accustomed to will inevitably involve the application of some tried-and-tested techniques.

Surprisingly few people are creative enough to know when and where to stick their nose in, let alone to see what's actually under it.

We can all go through life looking at the same things, but it takes a creative mind to discover in them new thoughts, directions, and applications.

The creative mind perceives and connects those things that are seemingly unconnected.

Creative inventions are like precious babies—they don't just happen, they are lovingly made. The world does not miss what is yet unborn.

When failing, it takes great creative character to try and try again.

Ideas are nothing more than dreams until one becomes brave enough to work them through.

Creative individuals mature with each failure and deal with success in a measured fashion.

To be successfully creative you must be prepared to knuckle down and never give up, to find courage when the odds are stacked against you, and to develop the patience to deal with your critics.

Those who achieve the most from their creative potential have three main things in common:
Enthusiasm;
An ability to trust their senses;
Dogged persistence.

A good mind is wasted
if it is not used well.

**Intelligence is a gift we enter the
world with. Fed and nourished by
experience, time, and curiosity, we
furnish it with knowing.**

Audacity is the historical cry
that has spurred on each new
advance and breakthrough in
science and the arts.

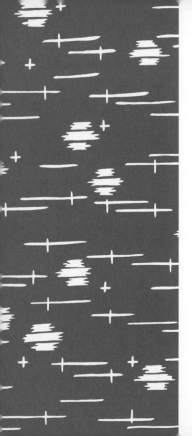

Too much wisdom is daily being buried alive in information.

What is the value of a single idea? Each is an acorn capable of producing a thousand forests.

Mankind is not disturbed by actual things—he is disturbed by the views he takes of them.

The cry goes out: "There must be a rational solution." Then commences the irrational process of trying to discover it.

**The more you think,
the more time you have.**

Henry Ford

Life is full of problems. With each one we solve we grow intellectually and creatively.

Umbilical cords are meant to be cut. Once free to explore and discover, the infant will still return to hold the hand of its mother.

A lifetime of experience may lead to a single moment of creative insight—and it will all have been worthwhile.

Rarely will one person tell another:
"I have changed."
But change is what they do.

**More often than not, when creative
ideas are turned into reality, there
is profit to be gained—spiritual,
emotional, intellectual, financial...
or all of these things.**

The creative mind is vigorous—it runs
in a permanent state of curiosity.
Deny it an outlet and it soars, unable to
land, like a winged eagle with no feet.

It is ideas that have shaped the course of history and it is ideas that will shape the course of the future.

When we change,
all life changes.

The most creative among us are those who have learned much from others.

That which is obvious is most
often the least understood.

**It takes great imagination to climb
onto the shoulders of giants in
order to see further than they did.**

Wild ideas are like wild horses—
it is easier to break in the one already
in the corral than to go chasing into
the unknown after another one.

The greatest creative joy is to begin.

To reach our creative state, with experience as our guide, we must be prepared to take the vital steps within ourselves, to journey deep into our subconscious to those areas that lie out of everyday reach. Here are the raw materials which, if we can reach them, find life as music, art, design, invention, or inspired thought.

A creative fool is the person who stands rooted to the spot, hoping not to get run over when he has discovered he is on the right track.

Persistence lies at a point beyond everything we have already tried, and all that we have already done.

Each new idea stretches our mind. It constantly expands and we are never the same as we were before.

Each creative challenge is like being tethered to a rope—we either climb it to the top and cut ourselves free, or we leave ourselves hung out to dry upon it.

The creative life appears to consist of discovering what it is you do best and then leaving it behind to try something entirely different.

Throughout time, throughout the world, countless others, intellectually equal to yourself, have creatively mastered problems just as baffling as those you now face.

With a creative outlook your entire life can be filled with revelation.

Most of us are content to wait until we are inspired before starting. Others start in the knowledge that action will always generate inspiration.

Happiness lies in the joy of achievement and the sheer thrill of creative effort.

The creative personality learns far more from pursuing false assumptions and making mistakes than from exposure to any font of wisdom.

The creative mind is like a life preserver: reassuring to know it's there, and at its best when we're floundering in the deep end.

Creative people are the masters of their minds, not mastered by their minds.

All serious daring begins from within.

Ideas may turn into magic, or they may turn into dust, but they never lead nowhere.

In the chronology of the world creation was around well before man created killing.

Creativity is a combination of working with the new and the already known to achieve a desired end.

Create a system or be enslaved by another's.

I will not reason and compare; my business is to create.

Creative sense is not always common sense.

To err is human but to really foul things up requires a computer.

We do not see the world as it is, we see it as we are.

It is not people that rule the world but thoughts. These are stronger than any material force. Thoughts rule the world, and the greatest of thinkers know this.

Do not accept trudging along through life never knowing what it is you are seeking.

Until we are prepared to throw away all we know and the constraints of conditioned thought, form will continue to follow function.

He who is most deaf is he who chooses not to hear.

Apprehension is a manifestation of intelligence. Creative ability is reserved for those who have within them the capacity to act with wisdom on that which they apprehend.

Creative ideas breed like rabbits— all one needs is a pretty pair to get the process rolling.

Each creative individual has within himself both teacher and pupil.

Tell a person to create and he'll try to solve the problem you have located. Teach a person to be creative and he'll not only help to solve problems, he'll help to locate them.

Better go home and make a net, rather than dive for fish at random.

Chinese proverb

Sir Isaac Newton famously said, "If I have seen further it is by standing on the shoulders of giants." But even a creative giant can be lifted further with the help of the shoulders of creative dwarves.

A work of art is a curious thing—a tool of communication in which the creator invests his integrity, intellect, understanding, and belief to put the message across. And once exhibited, depending upon how one looks at it, the message is either garbled, misunderstood, or crystal clear.

The creative world is divided into two sets of people—those who do, and those who would like to take the credit.

Creative people would rather spend half their life making mistakes than spend it doing nothing.

When you go to the fountain of knowledge do you drink or just gargle?

Creative people attract followers through inspiration and motivation, not morbid curiosity.

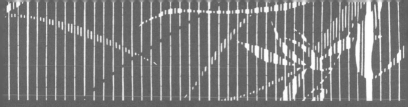

Creative people are often accused of having delusions of grandeur, often by people with delusions of adequacy.

God's greatest gift to a creative person is a thick skin.

Ideas are there to be embraced.
The shy will only live to see them dance away with a stranger.

When a person becomes known for their originality, it is something that will stick with them for the rest of their lives, like a marriage, for better or for worse, whether they like it or not.

It takes courage to live life creatively. It takes a strong person to retain his own individuality.

It is not because things are difficult that we do not dare; it is because we do not dare that things are difficult.

Seneca

We are all creative; life itself is an art. Our own life is our greatest work of art—a life of constant creation filled with infinite possibilities.

The creative view is that the world owes you nothing, and everything is a gift.

Life force is what we are born with, each of us transforms everything that is around us, all that touches our senses, our imaginations, thoughts, feelings, dreams, and aspirations into action…into expression…. How could any life therefore be anything other than unique?

The creative life brings all of its energy to each moment and every new encounter, ready to improvise when faced with the unexpected and inventing new scenarios as often as required.

What is art?
When you cannot find what you
mean anywhere around, create it—
and show it to others.

**What is usually revealed clearly in
creative practice is that its
research has been well concealed.**

Only the creative are truly free.

We will either find a way, or make one.

Hannibal

Throughout history it seems industry has advanced itself by creating new and more seductive ways of extending the number of important operations a workforce might perform without thinking about them.

Always remember that the same creative minds that are capable of the greatest virtues are also creatively capable of the greatest vices.

To be more creative one should simply choose to be. Then be. Then support everyone else in being.

We can all change ourselves. And when we do the world somehow changes too.

When we are capable of accepting the notions of dreaming, visualizing, and conceptualizing we can all work at what we currently do more creatively.

Every day there exist hundreds of possibilities to work at doing things more creatively.

To be a creative rebel is to attempt to bring about one's own individual creative freedom which, in turn, may contribute to the building of a freer world for everyone else.

Creative people are aware that there is a great deal of experimentation to be undertaken before they can even hope to make others accept their ideas.

The senses are the foundation of a creative life.

Creativity is a dynamic process that can be learned over time.

One is either balancing on the creative tightrope or waiting one's turn to mount it.

To become more creative one must first create one's inner life, for without it we are only slaves to our surroundings.

In the world of reality there are limits, but the world of creative imagination knows no bounds.

We must express ourselves creatively or miss the chance. Each of us is one of a kind, and our expression will either be allowed to exist through all time, or, if quelled, lost forever.

Everything that has been created has beauty, but not everyone is prepared to see it.

Creative discovery lies not over the horizon but in the landscape before us. It exists in our developing new ways of looking at it.

The beauty we love the most is the beauty that we love to create.

Creative people are the way they are because they are driven by the need to communicate, to share, and to make themselves understood. These things drive them more than any desire for respect or praise.

Imagination stirs the pond and it takes stillness for the muddy water to become clear.

The mind is not a vessel to be filled, but a fire to be ignited.

Plutarch

People are creatures of habit— they would prefer to face the same old problems than to consider new creative solutions.

Ask a creative person what they try to avoid most in life and they will tell you boredom.

It's a curious notion that the entire world can become shattered or transformed by a single creative thought.

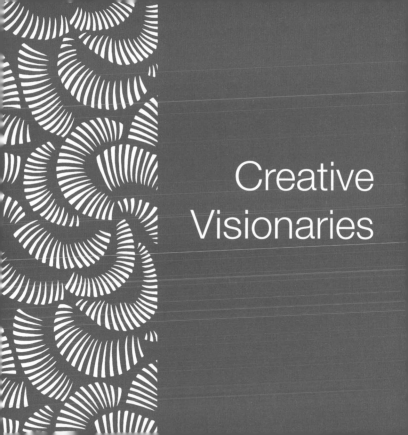

Creative
Visionaries

Whenever man comes up with a better mousetrap, nature immediately comes up with a better mouse.

James Carswell

It is not enough to have a good mind; the main thing is to use it well.

René Descartes

The man with a new idea is a crank—until the idea succeeds.

Mark Twain

The world we have made as a result of the level of thinking we have done thus far creates problems we cannot solve at the same level of thinking at which we created them.

Albert Einstein

I invent nothing.
I rediscover.

Auguste Rodin

I dream for a living.
Steven Spielberg

There are painters who transform the sun to a yellow spot, but there are others who with the help of their art and their intelligence transform a yellow spot into the sun.

Pablo Picasso

Every now and then go away, even briefly, have a little relaxation, for when you come back to your work your judgment will be surer; since to remain constantly at work will cause you to lose power.

Leonardo da Vinci

One must still have chaos in oneself to be able to give birth to a dancing star.

Friedrich Nietzsche

There is a right physical size for every idea.

Henry Moore

Anyone can look for history in a museum. The creative explorer looks for history in a hardware store.

Robert Wieder

Errors using inadequate data
are much less than those
using no data at all.

Charles Babbage

**Computers are useless. They can
only give you answers.**

Pablo Picasso

Genius is one percent inspiration, and ninety-nine percent perspiration.

Thomas A. Edison

I used to think anyone doing anything weird was weird. Now I know that it is the people that call others weird that are weird.

Paul McCartney

Greater than the tread of mighty armies is an idea whose time has come.

Victor Hugo

If at first the idea is not absurd, then there is no hope for it.

Albert Einstein

Talent is always conscious of its own abundance and does not object to sharing.

Alexander Solzhenitsyn

Change only
favors minds
that are
diligently
looking and
preparing for
discovery.
Louis Pasteur

A dwarf standing on the shoulders of a giant may see farther than the giant himself.

Robert Burton

The brain is a wonderful organ; it starts the moment you get up in the morning and does not stop until you get to the office.

Robert Frost

Reality is an illusion, albeit a very persistent one.

Albert Einstein

Youth is the period in which a man can be hopeless. The end of every episode is the end of the world. But the power of hoping through everything, the knowledge that the soul survives its adventures, that great inspiration comes to the middle-aged.

G. K. Chesterton

Enthusiasm is the inspiration of everything great. Without it no man is to be feared, and with it none despised.

Christian Nestell Bovee

I have a dream.
Martin Luther King

Great spirits have always encountered violent opposition from mediocre minds.

Albert Einstein

The torpid artist seeks inspiration at any cost, by virtue or by vice, by friend or by fiend, by prayer or by wine.

Ralph Waldo Emerson

Originality is nothing but judicious imitation.

Voltaire

Few people think more than two or three times a year. I've made an international reputation for myself by thinking once or twice a week.

George Bernard Shaw

The conventional army
loses if it does not win.
The guerrilla wins if they
do not lose.

Henry Kissinger

Computers in the future will weigh no more than 1.5 tons.

Popular Mechanics, **forecasting the advance of science in 1949**

In 1943 the then chairman of IBM famously predicted that in his estimation there was a world market for "maybe" five computers.

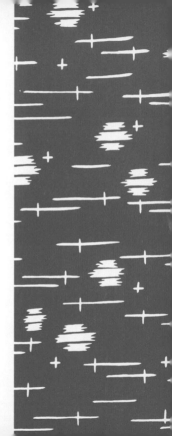

Who the hell wants to hear actors talk?

> attributed to H. M. Warner,
> Warner Brothers, 1927

We don't like their sound, and guitar music is on the way out.

> Decca Recording Company
> rejecting the Beatles, 1962

Everything that can be invented has been invented.

**Charles H. Duell,
US Office of Patents, 1899**

Louis Pasteur's theory of germs is ridiculous fiction.

Pierre Pachet, Professor of Physiology at Toulouse, 1872

Inventions have long since reached their limit, and I see no hope for further development.

**Julius Frontinus,
Roman engineer, first century A.D.**

Heavier-than-air flying machines
are impossible.

Lord Kelvin, President, Royal Society, 1895

It's not the critic who counts, not the one who points out how the strong man stumbled or how the doer of deeds might have done them better. The credit belongs to the man who is actually in the arena; whose face is marred with the sweat and dust and blood; who strives valiantly; who errs and comes up short again and again;

who knows the great enthusiasms,
the great devotions and spends
himself in a worthy cause and who,
at best knows the triumph of high
achievement and who at worst, if
he fails, at least fails while daring
greatly so that his place shall
never be with those cold and timid
souls who know neither victory
nor defeat.

Theodore Roosevelt

Don't tell my mother I'm in politics: she
thinks I play the piano in a whorehouse.

Mark Twain

I hear and I forget.
I see and I remember.
I do and I understand.

Confucius

I keep six honest serving-men,
(They taught me all I knew);
Their names are What and
   Why and When,
And How and Where and Who.

Rudyard Kipling

I strive to
be brief,
and I become
obscure.

Horace

It takes a lot of time to
be a genius; you have
to sit around so much
doing nothing, really
doing nothing.

Gertrude Stein

Everywhere I go I find a poet has been there before me.

Sigmund Freud

The spider's touch, how exquisitely fine! Feels at each thread, and lives along the line.

Alexander Pope

All art is but imitation of nature.

Seneca

Ah good taste! What a dreadful thing! Taste is the enemy of creativeness.

Pablo Picasso

My soul can find no staircase to heaven
unless it be through earth's loveliness.
Michelangelo

A beautiful form is better than a
beautiful face; it gives a higher
pleasure than statues or pictures;
it is the finest of the fine arts.
Ralph Waldo Emerson

Words are, of course, the most
powerful drug used by mankind.

Rudyard Kipling

**Man is a make-believe animal—
he is never so truly himself as when
he is acting a part.**

William Hazlitt

Life is not an exact science.
It is an art.

Samuel Butler

**The secret to creativity
is knowing how to hide
your sources.**

Albert Einstein

Creativity is a drug
I cannot live without.
Cecil B. DeMille

The test of a first-rate intelligence
is the ability to hold two opposed
ideas in the mind at the same
time, and still retain the ability
to function.

F. Scott Fitzgerald

Every child is an artist. The
problem is how to remain an
artist once he grows up.

Pablo Picasso

I would rather live in a world where my life is surrounded by mystery than live in a world so small that my mind could comprehend it.

Harry Emerson Fosdick

There is nothing new except what has been forgotten.

Marie Antoinette

Thank goodness I was never sent to school; it would have rubbed off some of the originality.

Beatrix Potter

Poetry is the art of creating imaginary gardens with real toads.

Marianne Moore

In a dark time, the eye begins to see.

Theodore Roethke

Every man's work, whether it be literature or music or pictures or architecture or anything else, is always a portrait of himself.

Samuel Butler

I do not know what I may appear to the world; but to myself I seem to have been only like a boy playing on the seashore, and diverting myself now and then finding a smoother pebble or a prettier shell than ordinary, whilst the great ocean of truth lay all undiscovered before me.

Sir Isaac Newton

That which builds is better than that which is built.

Ralph Waldo Emerson

He who wonders discovers that this in itself is wonder.

M. C. Escher

We see things as we are, not as they are.

Leo Rosten

It is worth mentioning, for future reference, that the creative power which bubbles so pleasantly in beginning a new book quiets down after a time, and one goes on more steadily. Doubts creep in. Then one becomes resigned. Determination not to give in, and the sense of an impending shape keep one at it more than anything.

Virginia Woolf

People should think things out fresh
and not just accept conventional
terms and the conventional way
of doing things.

R. Buckminster Fuller

**Creativity is the sudden
cessation of stupidity.**

Edwin H. Land

Invading armies can be resisted, but
not an idea whose time has come.

Victor Hugo

The quality of decision is like
the well-timed swoop of a
falcon which enables it to
strike and destroy its victim.

Sun Tzu

Every act of creation
is first of all an act
of destruction.

Pablo Picasso

The principle goal of education is to create men who are capable of doing new things, not simply of repeating what other generations have done—men who are creative, inventive, and discoverers.

Jean Piaget

My work is a game—a very serious game.

M. C. Escher

There is nothing in a caterpillar that tells you it's going to be a butterfly.

R. Buckminster Fuller

He that complies against his will is of his own opinion still.

Samuel Butler

The quicksilver of creativity will not be solidified by legal pronouncement; it will necessarily flow into new and sometimes frightening fields.

Judge Matthew Tobriner

Man is endowed with creativity in order to multiply that which has been given him; he has not created, but destroyed. There are fewer and fewer forests, rivers are drying up, wildlife has become extinct, the climate is ruined, and the earth is becoming ever poorer and uglier.

Anton Chekhov

Responsibility is what awaits outside the Eden of Creativity.

Nadine Gordimer

Only passions, and great passions, can raise the soul to great things. Without them there is no sublimity, either in morals or in creativity. Art returns to infancy and virtue becomes small-minded.

Denis Diderot

Creativity seems to emerge from multiple experiences, coupled with a well-supported development of personal resources, including a sense of freedom to venture beyond the known.

Loris Malaguzzi

The great challenge which faces us is to assure that, in our society of bigness, we do not strangle the voice of creativity, that the rules of the game do not come to overshadow its purpose, that the grand orchestration of society leaves ample room for the man who marches to the music of another drummer.

Hubert H. Humphrey

Whatever creativity is, it is in part a solution to a problem.

Brian Aldiss

Postmodernism entices us with the siren call of liberation and creativity, but it may be an invitation to intellectual and moral suicide.

Gertrude Himmelfarb

Advocating the mere tolerance of difference between women is the grossest reformism. It is a total denial of the creative function of difference in our lives. Difference must be not merely tolerated, but seen as a fund of necessary polarities between which our creativity can spark like a dialectic.

Audre Lorde

True creativity often starts where language ends.

Arthur Koestler

He who asks fortune-tellers the future unwittingly forfeits an inner intimation of coming events that is a thousand times more exact than anything they may say. He is impelled by inertia, rather than curiosity, and nothing is more unlike the submissive apathy with which he hears his fate revealed than the alert dexterity with which the man of courage lays hands on the future.

Walter Benjamin

Genius is no more than childhood recaptured at will, childhood equipped now with man's physical means to express itself, and with the analytical mind that enables it to bring order into the sum of experience, involuntarily amassed.

Charles Baudelaire

When you are listening to somebody, completely, attentively, then you are listening not only to the words, but also to the feeling of what is being conveyed, to the whole of it, not part of it.

Jiddu Krishnamurti

Ordinary people think that talent must be always on its own level and that it arises every morning like the sun, rested and refreshed, ready to draw from the same storehouse—always open, always full, always abundant—new treasures that it will heap up on those of the day before; such people are unaware that, as in the case of all mortal things, talent has its increase and decrease, and that independently of the career it takes, like everything that breathes…it undergoes all the accidents of health, of sickness, and of the dispositions of the soul—its gaiety or its sadness. As with our perishable flesh, talent is obliged constantly to keep guard over itself, to combat, and to keep perpetually on the alert amid the obstacles that witness the exercise of its singular power.

Eugène Delacroix

When you cannot make up your mind which of two evenly balanced courses of action you should take—choose the bolder.

William Joseph Slim

The mind, ever the willing servant, will respond to boldness, for boldness, in effect, is a command to deliver mental resources.

Norman Vincent Peale

Stand upright, speak thy thoughts, declare the truth thou hast, that all may share; Be bold, proclaim it everywhere: They only live who dare.

Lewis Morris

The march of invention has clothed mankind with powers of which a century ago the boldest imagination could not have dreamt.

Henry George

Flow with whatever is happening and let your mind be free. Stay centered by accepting whatever you are doing. This is the ultimate.

Chuang Tzu

If I have made any valuable discoveries, it has been owing more to patient attention than to any other talent.

Sir Isaac Newton

It is time for us all to stand and cheer for the doer, the achiever—the one who recognizes the challenges and does something about it.

Vince Lombardi

The best emotions to write out of are anger and fear or dread. The least energizing emotion to write out of is admiration. It is very difficult to write out of because the basic feeling that goes with admiration is a passive contemplative mood.

Susan Sontag

Our life is composed greatly from dreams, from the unconscious, and they must be brought into connection with action. They must be woven together.

Anaïs Nin

No one has ever written, painted, sculpted, modeled, built, or invented except literally to get out of hell.

Antonin Artaud

Concerning all acts of initiative and creation, there is one elementary truth the ignorance of which kills countless ideas and splendid plans: that the moment one definitely commits oneself, then providence moves too. All sorts of things occur to help one that would never otherwise have occurred. A whole stream of events issues from the decision, raising in one's favor all manner of unforeseen incidents, meetings, and material assistance which no man could have dreamed would have come his way.

Johann Wolfgang von Goethe

Be daring, be different, be impractical,
be anything that will assert integrity
of purpose and imaginative vision
against the play-it-safers, the
creatures of the commonplace,
the slaves of the ordinary.

Cecil Beaton

Imagination is the voice of
daring. If there is anything
Godlike about God it is that.
He dared to imagine everything.

Henry Miller

Great minds are related to the brief span of time during which they live as great buildings are to a little square in which they stand: you cannot see them in all their magnitude because you are standing too close to them.

Arthur Schopenhauer

The spirited horse, which will try to win the race of its own accord, will run even faster if encouraged.

Ovid

**It is either easy
or impossible.**
Salvador Dalí

Art has to move you
and design does not,
unless it's a good
design for a bus.
David Hockney

**A good composer
does not imitate;
he steals.**
Igor Stravinsky

Don't listen to those who say, "you're taking too big a chance." Michelangelo would have painted the Sistine floor, and it would surely be rubbed out by today. Most important, don't listen when the little voice of fear inside you rears its ugly head and says they're all smarter than you out there. They're more talented, they're taller, blonder, prettier, luckier, and they have connections. I firmly believe that if you follow a path that interests you, not to the exclusion of love, sensitivity, and cooperation with others, but with the strength of conviction that you can move others by your own efforts, and do not make success or failure the criteria by which you live, the chances are you'll be a person worthy of your own respect.

Neil Simon

Those who do not want to imitate anything, produce nothing.

Salvador Dalí

When I judge art, I take my painting and put it next to a God-made object like a tree or flower. If it clashes, it is not art.

Marc Chagall

The barriers are not erected which can say to aspiring talents and industry, "Thus far and no farther."

Ludwig van Beethoven

Be great in act, as you have been in thought.

William Shakespeare

A desire arises in the mind. It is satisfied, immediately another comes. In the interval which separates two desires a perfect calm reigns in the mind. It is at this moment freed from all thought, love, or hate. Complete peace equally reigns between two mental waves.

Sri Swami Sivananda

Artists to my mind are the real architects of change, and not the political legislators who implement change after the fact.

William S. Burroughs

Do not try to push your way through to the front ranks of your profession; do not run after distinctions and rewards; but do your utmost to find an entry into the world of beauty.

Konstantin Stanislavsky

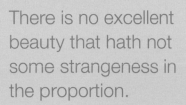

There is no excellent beauty that hath not some strangeness in the proportion.

Francis Bacon

It is only in our decisions that we are important.

Jean-Paul Sartre

That must be wonderful; I have no idea of what it means.

Albert Camus

Fashion is something barbarous, for it produces innovation without reason and imitation without benefit.

George Santayana

Innovation! One cannot be forever innovating. I want to create classics.

Coco Chanel

We live at a time when man believes
himself fabulously capable of creation,
but he does not know what to create.

José Ortega y Gasset

**The mind loves the unknown.
It loves images whose meaning is
unknown, since the meaning of the
mind itself is unknown.**

René Magritte

All in all, the creative act is not performed by the artist alone; the spectator brings the work in contact with the external world by deciphering and interpreting its inner qualifications and thus adds his contribution to the creative act.

Marcel Duchamp

Musings

Today and down through the ages man has turned again and again to his muses for inspiration and creative guidance—sometimes to the traditionally famous nine muses of Ancient Greece, or where they prove too elusive to his needs, he has created his own.

Whether we find inspiration wandering "lonely as a cloud" or by immersing ourselves in the urban jungle, each of us has somewhere we tend to or prefer to turn to for inspiration.

Creative people learn to replenish themselves with the aid of their inner and external muses.

A hushed and unhurried walk through galleries brimming with art can fuel the creativity of any person who gives themselves over to the experience.

I often turn to music for inspiration, and to fresh coffee, and I meditate—or I get back to nature, or head for the bustling city streets.

Go down to the sea where creative problems are one drop in an ocean of possibilities.

Whether you find inspiration sailing along the Grande Canal of Venice or submerging yourself in the graphics of a computer game you soon get to know who and what your muses are.

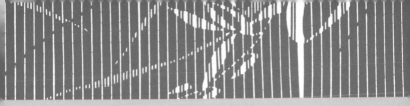

Our muses are associated with more than one would imagine—music and nature, healing, astronomy, celebration, tragedy, comedy—every form of inspiration imaginable.

Why do we create? Because we want to. Ask me why and I shall tell you: it is because we must.

Through our creativity we cultivate our most enduring relationships.

We turn to our muses to recover our inspiration or to rekindle our passion for what we are creating.

Clio is the muse to call upon for historical and heroic poetry. Often depicted with a set of tablets or a scroll it was she who introduced the Phoenician alphabet into Greece.

Euterpe is the goddess of memory and a muse of music and lyric poetry, joy, and pleasure. Her very name translates as "delight" or "rejoicing." She is depicted with the double flute.

Erato is the muse of lyric poetry and mimicry, depicted carrying a lyre. We turn to her for inspiration with love poetry and the erotic.

Melpomene is the muse of tragedy, represented wearing a tragic mask. She is often depicted holding a mask in one hand and a knife or a club in the other.

Polyhymnia is the long-cloaked muse of sacred hymn, eloquence, and dance. She is mostly presented in a pensive or meditative pose against a pillar or holding a finger up to her lips.

Thalia is the muse who presides over rural pursuits, comedy, and pastoral poetry. She bears a comic mask and a shepherd's crook.

Terpsichore is the muse of the dramatic chorus and dancing, hence the dance term "terpsichorean." She is usually depicted seated with a lyre.

The ancient muse of eloquence is Calliope or Calliopeia—armed with her emblems of a stylus and wax tablets, we turn to this distinguished, beautiful-voiced muse to inspire epic or heroic poetry.

Creativity is a spiritual path to which we become devoted, or an ocean in which we immerse ourselves.

Creativity is the search for inspiration, passion, and meaning.

A life without creativity is one of restlessness, of being unsatisfied, a deep-rooted feeling of never reaching fulfillment. We must be creative.

During periods of creativity, however long the exercise, we feel complete and contented in "doing."

When a creative person stops being creative a feeling of emptiness soon returns, and each moment becomes one of questioning who we are, and our purpose in this life.

Why must we be creative? Because there is no better thing to do. Because we were born with the capacity to question and the desire for answers.

As we grow and age we lament having lost touch with the dreams and fantasies of childhood. Suddenly we experience a lack of meaning to our life—but when we discover our creativity, the pleasurable experiences of our past come rushing back and suddenly our life is filled with meaning.

When we hold the key to our creativity we are only ever a few small steps away from realizing everything we believed possible.

How can anyone be expected to be creative when they feel unfulfilled, harassed, restless, or burned out? Confronted with a sea of possibilities such people just stand hoping that one day their ship will come in.

Our own negative attitude is the assassin of our inspiration.

When we work for too long our body and our mind become weary, our hearts grow heavy, and we feel uninspired. When we are being creative the opposite happens.

Why do we need our muses? Because inspiration does not simply happen — we tend to block its channels with our own negativity.

Before we can begin to create we must first create the right internal and external conditions which will fuel our creativity.

Creativity is not necessarily a form of bravery. Many top creative people live their lives in fear and terror, but being frightened never seems to stop them from doing the things they set out to do.

There can be no creativity where there is no care.

If we are not prepared to listen or to come into contact with our sources of inspiration, the muses will remain unheard or out of reach, and our creativity will remain elusive.

Creativity is something we must want to experience. It involves great enlivening choices—life choices, life wishes—we must be prepared to make.

There is only one sure way to dispel our fear of change—it is to seek out our muses and reach for our deepest inspiration. Soon fear will segue with desire.

Our muses live mainly within us and take their own personal forms. When we connect with them we connect back with our essential life force.

Creative people are often accused of being locked in a fruitless search to discover the meaning of life. But in truth they are locked in the fruitful discovery of experiencing being truly alive.

When we embrace our visions our muses awaken.

Our muses present us with the sacred silence from which music is born.

To search for your muses close your eyes and look deep inside you. Allow your search to carry you back into your past—they may exist in that place where we store our visions of the future, they may come to us in a dream, or appear in the instant that we open our eyes.

In that first moment of any form of creativity we suddenly feel whole, connected, and inspired.

Our creative muses don't teach us anything, they only help us to find what there is already within ourselves.

The only way out of creativity is to go through it.

Only when we can reach our inner creative resources at will can we begin to live a creative life on our own terms.

Our creativity helps us to clear our mind and create more balance in our life.

When creativity eludes us it is because we are thinking only with our mind. The situation will only change when we begin to think also with our heart and our spirit.

Our creative muse is that thing which truly inspires us to listen to our heart.

Our muses urge us to try to be mindful, and to let things take their natural course.

When we can connect with our creative muse, no matter what our surroundings, our mind can become still and clear.

Our creativity allows us to see the nature of all things clearly.

The deeper into creativity we immerse ourselves, the lonelier you would imagine it would become, but deep in there we are in the inspiring company of many muses, and it is suddenly the least lonely of places to be.

Many strange and wondrous things come and go, and some are found and others lost forever.

Creativity is a peeling away of the layers of the heart to become free and open even in the face of opposition.

Creativity is there for everyone, for everyone in their own way is original, and each has something important to do or to say.

No matter how attuned we may become with our surroundings and the world around us, each time we embark upon a creative journey that takes us into our inner world we will always discover new territory.

Creativity encourages us to be reckless, to be careless, to be anything we like—only to do it creatively.

Our creative muses save us from perfectionism and put us instead on the path to playful invention.

All creativity is based upon our most fundamental human need, which is to know oneself deeply and in relation to the rest of the world.

Our creative muses lead us gently by the hand away from those things we have tried and failed in, and point us in the direction of what it is still possible for us to do.

Seek perfection too soon in the creative process and you're likely to end up with a perfect failure instead of a rough but workable model.

The greatest creative discovery any of us can make is that we can all alter our lives by altering our state of mind.

All the reasons in the world why you cannot do something can be effectively outweighed by a single reason why you can—all that is required is to create that reason.

The creative person must never give up their right to be wrong, for it is through this right that we develop our ability to learn new things and move life forward.

Creativity is the only place a person may fly unaided—here we may soar with the eagles and dine on clouds.

New ideas are like untried skyrockets—some fly straight and true and reach for the stars, and others go up a few feet then come down again with a loud bang.

With creative freedom there is no voice to tell us that we cannot possibly do the things that we are doing. This leaves us the possibility of discovering that what we believed to be impossible is possible, or vice versa.

To be creative one should confront one's fears and doubts. These are human traits and only by allowing oneself the right to be human can one become a happier and more creatively productive person.

Our creative muses encourage us to bring out the best in ourselves, which is all well and nice provided that being our best does not bring out the worst in us.

The alchemy of creativity is being able to turn a messy first draft into the perfect result.

Attempts at instant creativity are like stepping out into the pitch darkness of the unknown. One can proceed in the hope there's a floor to walk on, but it would be prudent to take along a parachute.

Have perseverance as your muse:
Our greatest glory is not in never falling,
but in rising every time we fall.

Confucius

Have respect as your muse:
If you treat an individual…as if he
were what he ought to be and
could be, he will become what he
ought to be and could be.

Johann Wolfgang von Goethe

When we have potential as our muse we
will never become "has-beens" but go
through our creative lives as "will-bes."

Teach me the reason for inspiration being or not being, and I shall have learned to fly.

Possibly the most fragile thing is inspiration. It may come in the glimpsing of a newborn baby or fledgling, a gentle breeze that touches your cheek, a color, taste, touch, or smell. It comes to us in what sometimes seems an eternity and can be gone again in an instant.

An uninspired thought is as easy to lift off the ground as a shadow.

Every single day there is new beauty everywhere, just waiting to be born.

The greatest inspiration we can offer to a creative spirit is the spiritual inspiration that comes when they discover that we believe in them and that we are willing to trust their creativity.

Any person may go from this life "accomplished" who has left the world a little better than it was before with their creativity.

We are all creatively equal, we are all just one dream away from creative genius.

Creativity and vision can transform a pile of rocks into a cathedral.

Someone else's muse may well come along and give them a bigger idea than yours. But your idea is unique. There will never be another like it, and its time will come.

The truly creative people out there have the ability to make us feel that we too can become truly creative.

Aim for creative achievement. It is far more satisfying than success, and anyway, success always follows achievement.

Sometimes one has to go out on a creative limb and hang there by the fingernails.

There is no creative muse who would inspire anyone to slouch back in their chair, sigh a sigh of defeat, and make a wish that things would change.

The first creative discovery worth making is that we are not God. Creativity doesn't happen to us, we go out and make creativity happen to other things.

Time passes. It is up to each of us to make the best creative use of it we can.

When you next converse with your muses, ask them this: "Are you the kind of person who has the power to do creatively what no one else has the power to do?" If you come away inspired with a head full of ideas then chances are you are a creative genius.

One cannot create on doubt—it is like trying to go up by going down.

Creative people have the same ordinary qualities as everybody else, except that they have developed those ordinary qualities to a more than ordinary degree.

There is no philosophy available that will help a person to become creative when they insist on always doubting their ability to do so.

Good creativity takes as long as it takes.

Let enthusiasm become your muse—be enthusiastic and faithful in your creativity and you will always accomplish your objectives.

Our muses are our guiding spirits, our sources of inspiration. They help to point us in the right direction—but it is up to us, in this real world, to discover the path of least resistance.

To become a creative person a good starting point is to imagine yourself as being one.

**Nature creates
nothing uselessly.**

We can turn to the same muses over
and over again, for each time we ask
them how we might boost our creativity
the answer will depend on our situation
now, on what we are creating now, the
how and why of what we are involved
in at this moment.

**Let nature and her seasons
become your muse.**

Let potential be your muse. Do not dwell upon your frustrations—instead focus upon your unfulfilled potential.

Let chance be your muse. Ask any creative individuals where their information came from and they will tell you that the vast majority of it they stumbled upon along the way to seeking something else.

Let risk be your muse. The greatest risk to creativity is to not risk anything.

Let fun be your muse. Get away from everything, spend a day at the funfair or the seaside. Allow yourself to play again, to be thrilled again, to touch fear and sense excitement, and translate it back into your creative endeavors.

Let blankness be your muse. Meditate while staring at a blank wall, a blank book, a blank page. Watch a blank video, listen to the silence.

Let the moon be your muse, but when you point your finger at it try to look beyond the nail.

When confronted with the choice between two evils the majority will choose the lesser of the two. The creatively adventurous among us will opt for the one they've never tried before.

Never set out seeking perfection. The cobbler doesn't shine his shoes before he's created them.

Creativity lives on the opposite side of the fence to its neighbor cynicism.

When faced with things that appear hopeless, creativity becomes determined to make them otherwise.

Do not be guided by your fears, instead consult your dreams and your hopes.

When stuck for a creative idea ponder what areas of life you have yet to explore.

The path to our muse is via the heart.

What better life-wish could there be than to discover our creativity, to cultivate our creativity, and then to live from our creativity.

When we are stuck for a muse there are always people, places, and possibilities to turn to.

Creativity is better served by developing the gift of fantasy than by going through life absorbing positive knowledge.

Creativity awakens us to new forms of meaning. It is a mistake to restrict our association with creativity just to the arts or business—creativity is an entire approach to living a stimulating and rewarding life.

Wherever we may look, we will be able to find that which nourishes us, inspires us, and deepens our creative experience.

Creativity, whether in a group, an individual exercise, or a multinational project—from arranging a vase filled with flowers to coordinating a global experience—comes down to two key words: meaningful interaction.

It is said that one can instantly recognize when our muse arrives, for the moment we make contact through our creativity a shiver runs down our spine, tears may well up in our eyes, or the hairs on our body may stand on end.

To contact your muse think back and recall those times in which you have felt most creative, most alive, and call to mind the kind of experience that most inspired you. When we can identify the types of experiences that most inspired us in life we can concentrate upon creating more of these kinds of experiences.

When we are with our muse, all we need to do is close our eyes and anything becomes possible.

There is little room for imagination in a tidy mind. Creativity thrives on disorder.

You are a child of God. Your playing small doesn't serve the world. There is nothing enlightened about shrinking so that other people will not feel insecure around you. We were born to make manifest the glory of God that is within us. It isn't just in some of us, it is in everyone and as we let our own light shine, we unconsciously give others permission to do the same. As we are liberated from our own fear, our presence automatically liberates others.

Marianne Williamson

Workshops
and Creative
Benchmarks

It is always good when one feels a lack of inspiration to reflect upon those who had inspired ideas before us—inspiration is cross feeding.

Do not imagine that those great inventions and masterpieces of art came about with no effort at all. Even if, like Paul McCartney who composed the song "Yesterday," your best idea comes to you in a dream, you must be prepared to give yourself over to the dream and follow it through.

For generations the stalks of the sugar cane harvest were burned off as rubbish. Only recently did someone with a bit of creative imagination suggest it could be used as a fuel to generate electricity.

When I asked a very clever friend of mine what he was working on, he said, "a device to record aircraft engine vibration and play it back via a headrest," which has the effect of removing the vibration and noise encountered by passengers of air travel.

Somebody sat down and thought that if one was to take waste wood and break it down further into chips, they could restructure it into one of the most universally used building materials today—chipboard.

In medicine, someone once had the creative insight to lower the patient's body temperature in order to slow down the metabolism during surgical operations.

The way of creative progress is neither swift nor easy.

Every really new idea looks crazy at first.

Following a failure, those in a creative team with clear consciences are the ones suffering from memory loss.

Sense is not common.

Deep-sea divers have been able to reach previously prohibitive depths because someone thought about adding helium to their oxygen.

In 1980, I purchased what was then a revolutionary mini stereo cassette recorder/player. While I was enjoying it on a flight to Australia, I remarked to my wife how wonderful it would be if one day there could be something the same size fitted in the headrest in front of you on which you could view in-flight movies of your choice. Well, hindsight is always 20:20.

Who first had the thought of starting a forest backfire to put out a forest fire?

The only thing we can create
by resisting change is sorrow.

**Who first considered adding a
thermostatic device that on
reaching a certain point would be
able to switch the heat source off
and on again and so maintain a
constant temperature?**

We don't lose points for
adapting other people's ideas.

How many fingers were burned before someone dreamed up the oven mitt?

Creative inventions find their time. Leonardo da Vinci's drawings for what were originally considered outrageous designs have only recently been put to the test. His manned flying machine did in fact outfly the craft created by the Wright brothers, his clockwork car actually worked, and his mega crossbow really fired.

How many loose papers were flying around before someone had the creative insight to bend some wire into a paper clip to hold them together?

Was bouquet garni invented for its pleasing looks, wonderful aroma, its culinary value—or all three?

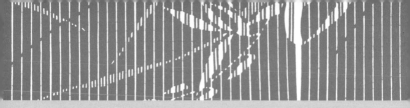

Who first had the idea of picking flowers and placing them on display inside the home?

What cook would be without the self-cleaning oven someone so kindly created for them?

In creative processes one must become daring if things are to become less difficult.

Sometimes the most creative thing we can do is to simplify the overcomplicated.

Creative goals are merely dreams with a plan and a deadline attached to them.

There is a proverb that says: the marksman hits the target partly by pulling, partly by letting go. And the boatsman reaches dry land partly by pulling, partly by letting go.

Teach yourself to free your mind from conventional thinking by introducing conceptualizing into your creative toolbox.

In projects that require group creativity the creative energy of youth is best balanced with the creative wisdom of age.

Set yourself some thought exercises:
How might you go about using waste resources to create something new—a material, a work of art or energy? Visualize the project through. Nurture your idea—this means trying to improve upon it, so objectively evaluate the idea and be prepared to reject that which does not work.

EXERCISE

In a group, have some creative fun by placing a wooden chair in the center of a circle and take turns transforming it into other uses. Don't go for the obvious, i.e. never a seat, but play it like a trombone; use it as a fishing rod, a cell phone, or a telescope.

EXERCISE

Create a stockpile of materials and simple basic tools and use the concept of bricolage to resolve a creative problem using only these items. The crew of Apollo 13 used this creative process, using just what was at hand to save their lives.

EXERCISE

In a group, use only
yourselves to physically
create different objects
and forms: statues,
classical and abstract;
animated machines;
animals or well-known
structures.

EXERCISE

1. In a group, begin walking in a circle around a large enough space, someone leading you through the terrain. Let go of the outside world and explore walking on ice, deep mud, through the waves, on eggshells, and broken glass.

2. Still walking, imagine a journey through a forest, enjoy imagining the smells, the sounds, those things that might startle you, such as a bird exploding into flight, a shotgun being fired, a tiger growling somewhere in the undergrowth. Take time.

3. Still walking, imagine external forces and their effect upon you as you move, like something pushing you from behind, something pulling you from the knees, the ankles, or the forehead.

EXERCISE

In a group, consider this: the Aboriginal Australians can vocally create everything in their world. Explore this. Recreate vocally the sounds of your world using your mind to imagine what it is you are recreating. Be as accurate as possible.

EXERCISE

Explore temperatures with the imagination: imagine cold and its effects upon the body, the voice, the breathing, and movement. Consider extreme heat, imagine a desert, being thirsty, exhausted from the heat, and the effort of moving under such extremes.

EXERCISE

Take a pencil and paper. Now draw a line.
What does it become and what does it tell you?
Does it suggest other forms? A crossing point,
a boundary, a new beginning?

EXERCISE

1. In a group, use a large flip chart and get someone to draw a simple form on it—a line, a circle, whatever comes to mind—then without discussing or criticizing, go around the group and list all the ideas that come up in a brainstorming session.

2. With the list of ideas, concepts, and possibilities that emerge, go around the group again and extend the possibilities even further and see what emerges. When the possibilities have been exhausted move onto the next person drawing a form to kick off another round. It needn't always be a form, it might also be a word.

In a good brainstorming session it has been known for a small group of people to become locked for hours generating extraordinary ideas from a simply drawn straight line.

When a group has been able to select among all the ideas generated and to embrace one, the first step to making decisions has been made.

EXERCISE

1. In a group, sit at a table and place a small amount of money in the center. Take turns making a small statement of what it might buy and why.

2. Still at the table, get everyone to empty their pockets of money and combine it to discover a total value of the pile. Go around the circle again and make short statements of what it might buy and why.

3. Still at the table, consider the combined amount of money and take turns making a statement of how to maximize it and possibly profit from its use.

4. Still at the table with the total combined money in front of you, brainstorm an idea: how one might finance a new car with what is on the table; how one might save a country with the amount. List each idea as it arrives, never discussing, never throwing away, and never criticizing another's contribution.

EXERCISE

Form a circle of people and get someone to go into the center and present a simple mime of an everyday occurrence, for example ironing a shirt. When asked by the next person in the circle, "What are you doing?" present a false answer, for example "downhill skiing." The next person steps in to replace the first and mimes downhill skiing, then provides another unexpected answer. And so on around the circle.

EXERCISE

1. In a group, write a list of things that have human connections, such as teeth, or love.

Brainstorm new ideas for new products that might help or celebrate these things. List them.

2. Continuing with the list of new products, take turns to vote for the best, most effective, most marketable, or most aesthetically pleasing and see which become the popular choice.

3. Develop the popular choice and have as a constraint the sum figure of the combined amount of money you discovered earlier and see if the group can work together to explore all the possibilities of creating and marketing the new thing.

EXERCISE

In a group, each person should
write the name of an object on
a flip chart, such as a bridge, a
house, a car, and so forth. Place
an object, perhaps a plank of
wood, in the center of a circle.
Starting with the first word on
the list go around the circle with
the brief of how one might create
the bridge with the plank of wood
being the central, most vital, and
most featured aspect of it. Then
the house, then the car...

EXERCISE

1. In a group, work in isolated spaces around a room as individuals. Someone should propose a fuse word—kitchen, vacation, health, or fun. Then each make a list of 50 words that spring to mind after a period of consideration linked to the fuse word.

2. Armed with your lists, come together as a group again. The first person should read out their list and the others should tick any words that match the reader's list. Then the second person reads what remains of their list and so forth around the circle, to the end.

EXERCISE

1. In a group, over the space of a one-hour lunchbreak, with a small, set amount of money, go out and find something to eat and the materials to create a gift for Mother's Day/the birth of a child/a wedding present. Dedicate enough time in the afternoon for people to make their gifts.

2. When the making period has ended, each maker should present their gift along with a short, sincere poem. It must really push home the event celebrated and have a high perceived value.

EXERCISE

1. Break a larger group into smaller working parties of three or four people. Distribute different newspapers to each group and allow a short amount of time for them to locate a story that they will turn into a short drama.

2. Armed with their newspaper stories each group goes away from the others to devise and rehearse their little play (which shouldn't depend on words.) After a fixed creation period, the groups come together to present their stories for the others who must attempt to decipher from the performance they've seen, the story that gave rise to it.

EXERCISE

Imagine holding an orange. Consider its shape, size, weight, and smell. Using precise hand movements, go through the mechanics of peeling it with care, imagining the juices, the segments, and the process of eating it, allowing memory and experience to inform your actions.

EXERCISE

Using a pencil and paper, sketch from memory a person you know; a place you have been; or a structure you have seen. Try to capture faithfully the essence of what is being drawn.

EXERCISE

Sift through a catalog or magazine and tear out a pile of ten or so advertisements or designs that work for you, and a pile of ten or so that you feel miss the mark. From the scraps you have compiled, try to analyze what it is that makes some work and others not.

EXERCISE

Look around your own life and your own home. Ponder the choices you have made. Why did you choose those pictures for your wall? What made you adopt that decoration or style? Be objective and don't shy away from being critical.

EXERCISE

Take a trip to a gallery or exhibition and find out
what stands out from everything else and leaves
a lasting impression on you. What is it about
these pieces that appeals to you?

Perhaps the greatest gifts
to creativity are time,
problems, and deadlines.

EXERCISE

Find within your lifestyle a small cross section of things that impress you. It may be your can opener, a piece of sculpture, an antique, or an appliance. Consider the design and the execution that went into each, and the creativity that made them exist.

EXERCISE

Go back to making lists. If you had the creative freedom and correct resources available to you what would you create or have created for you? Think each through from the conception of the idea to its execution.

EXERCISE

Whether it is a simple table ornament or entire ambience for a room, explore and celebrate a season, for example Christmas, using the less obvious things you find in place of store-bought solutions. Use greenery, fire, scents, and sounds, and experiment with your creativity.

The view from the outside is that the life of a creative person is limited, but rest assured that ability will never catch up with the world's demand for it. There will always be another level to rise to, and always somewhere for one's creativity to go next.

Creative work is the presentation of one's creative capabilities.

Create as you would wish and you will die happy.

Learn to understand instead of immediately judging.

Ponder this: each day we grow happy
in the knowledge that we do not know
where our creative limits lie.

**Every creative day is the portal of
new revelations and new discovery.**

Start each day afresh:
Create a new breakfast routine
Create a new look for yourself
Create a new route to work, or a new
working environment
Create new ways of communicating,
meeting, and socializing.

EXERCISE

Stand on one leg and with your arms, hands, free leg, head, and body, explore the limits of the immediate sphere that is around you. How far can you reach in any given direction while remaining balanced on one leg?

The very worst thing we can do is forget our creative mistakes. They are brimming over with information that will serve us well in everything we create from that time forward.

Creative thinking allows us to define problems and swiftly assimilate all the relevant data. It is a process of conceptualizing and reorganizing the information we collate, providing the springboard for deductive and inductive action.

Past misfortunes are deposits made in our bank of creative fortitude.

Action springs from our readiness to accept creative responsibility.

When we reduce stress from creative problem-solving and face it in a relaxed ambience it allows us to use a far larger area of the brain for the process at hand. The result is the swifter generation of more and superior ideas and a marked decrease in creative conflict.

Very nearly everyone has the capacity to be a creative thinker and to generate ideas that are original and meet with some standard of value.

Many have had their greatness made for them by their creative mistakes.

One should take creativity everywhere. Be creative even with leisure, as this is the place to hatch new thoughts.

Remember, when we create new thoughts, we create a new world for ourselves.

No matter how successful the execution on any creative journey, one must always bookend the stretch between planning and evaluation, or be in danger of remaining middle of the road.

No route has meaning in itself. It is a line that connects two or more points. Creativity with no point is a meaningless journey and a complete waste of time.

Ponder the imponderable. This is how to reach the height of creativity.

The possibilities of creative effort are stupendous and awe-inspiring.

It was a wise person who said, "When in charge, ponder. When in trouble, delegate. And when in doubt, mumble."

Create the self that you will be happy to live with your entire life. Then you can begin to trust your own creative judgement.

Create a good impression with the "you" that you have created.

When we create, we do so out of our own experience and understanding of life.

Mankind's propensity toward violence is a manifestation of his desire to create perhaps better conditions, or perhaps a better society. But because we don't know how to use our energy creatively we do the opposite and become destructive.

With creativity one can have everything the heart desires.

Every human being
has within him the
power to create and
the power to destroy.

**The nonexistent is not
necessarily absent due to lack of
sufficient desire for it. It is more
often because our desires in life
are not always matched by our
creative aptitude.**

Ever since man found that he needed to think in order to survive, he's been confronted by his own creativity. Our prehistoric ancestors found tools and weapons in stones and bones, the ability to use friction to create fire, fire to forge metal, metal to chisel out sculptures—and onward and upward.

When we create new wants we must also create the means of satisfying them.

We create in order to create a response, even if it is only our own.

A creative business creates customers.

Difficulty always creates opportunities.

Why conform? One comes into this life free and equal so why throw this to the wind by spending one's life trying to create a life that is just like everyone else's?

Why fear creativity? That which man's mind can create will always remain within the realms of man's character to control. This is creativity's most frightening, and most reassuring, aspect.

You can dream,
create, design,
and build the most
wonderful place
in the world, but
it requires people
to make the dream
a reality.

Walt Disney

Creativity must have its contrast.
In a painting there can be no light
without shade; music needs silence;
a cut diamond is always displayed on
dark velvet; and creativity needs
periods of noncreativity.

What would night be had man not created the lamp?

What use would clay be if man had not
created cups and jugs, and sculpture
and building materials?

Nature may have created deserts and forests and mountains, but it is man who created the orchards, the gardens, and the groves.

Mankind took a handful of sand and saw in it glass.

Mankind saw diseases and created cures, saw poisons and created antidotes.

Mankind sees systems and sets about creating new ones to avoid becoming a slave to another's.

People tend to view creative people as dreamers living in a dreamworld and accuse them of being unable to face reality. But the fundamental difference between the critic and the creator is that the creative person can turn one world into the other.

**To replicate is human,
to create, divine.**

The thing is to cross the line and create something with intent. Create something that has a unique place, function, or purpose in your life.

When we develop the ability to apply our mental and physical abilities to a single problem incessantly without becoming wearied or bored, we will have developed the first requisite for successful creativity.

**Too scared to be creative?
Ask anyone who is creating,
and they'll tell you that they
are scared too.**

Discipline is implicit in creative thinking,
along with perseverance that we might
keep the mind focused on one aspect
of a problem at a time. It is a mistake
to underestimate how difficult creativity
can be for even the most talented
among us when they are not familiar
with a thinking style that is imposed
upon a project.

Sometimes the best creative decision will be to borrow ideas from others, to reach innovation by reinventing where invention is necessary.

The essence of creativity is coming to terms with the "me" that we each are, of taking comfort from the things that "me" can do, and developing the confidence and skills to do the things that "me" would like to do.

The environment we find ourselves in is in part a direct result of the creative decisions we have made.

One enters the realm of creative thought without a set of prior expectations—without "oughts" and without "shoulds." What is essential to take into the process, especially if working in a group situation, is complete openness and trust.

461

Creativity should always aim for greatness—aim high and your best shot will have greatness to it. Aim too low and your arrow will almost always miss the target.

Good creative thinkers have the ability to locate and extract necessary information from a mass of stimuli. Enter into creativity without too many pre-existing concepts. This allows you to expand your perception beyond your established thinking patterns and notice what might otherwise be missed.

The brain and its processes instinctively set out to find familiar paths and past similarities to current problems. Creativity demands that we work beyond these constraints and constantly adapt our thinking to invent new ways.

Creative thinking is needed to prepare us to live in this rapidly changing world. Facts are not enough, nor are prior learned techniques. We need to be able to develop our creativity so it may keep pace and deal with change as and when it occurs.

First published by MQ Publications Limited
12 The Ivories, 6–8 Northampton Street
London N1 2HY
email: mail@mqpublications.com
website: www.mqpublications.com

Copyright © 2004 MQ Publications Limited
Text © 2004 David Baird

Design: Philippa Jarvis

ISBN: 1-84072-731-4

10 9 8 7 6 5 4 3 2 1

Printed and bound in China